Simon Schott

PLAY PIANO BY EAR

D0879135

An Easy Method for Playing Songs Without Reading Music

www.schott-music.com

Mainz · London · Madrid · New York · Paris · Prague · Tokyo · Toronto

Dedicated to
Jeannette Weiss
in gratitude

ED 9280
ISBN 978-3-7957-5519-5
© 2002 Schott Music GmbH & Co. KG, Mainz
Titelfoto: Bavaria Bildagentur, München
Printed in Germany · BSS 50141

CONTENTS

The Fascination of Playing Piano By Ear

I remember my first secret excursion into the night-life of my home town; which as a seventeen-year-old school boy I financed by sawing boards in a brick factory. I was drawn by a magic power to a bar in the cellar of an otherwise very respectable house where a blue neon sign blinked every two seconds with the name 'Atlantic Bar'.

This bar had nothing disreputable about it. A woman in her thirties, dressed in a high-necked evening gown, sat at the piano, playing without a single sheet of music in front of her. She played all the beautiful standards I knew, and even more beautiful ones that I didn't. The customers relived the pleasant memories of happy times, while I sat for hours over my outrageously expensive glass of apple juice, unable to take my eyes off her. I was head-over-heels in love.

Today, I can't quite remember what she looked like. But certainly she had no more than a perfectly ordinary face. The cause of my fascination can only have been the irresistible enchantment of her piano playing. I'm sure if she had been a bus conductor or a drawing teacher I wouldn't have paid her the slightest notice.

A Parisian friend of mine once expressed the fascination of improvised piano music in other words. We were strolling down to Place de la Trinité, at two in the morning, when we came abreast of the open door of a small bar, out of which came the sound of fairly decent piano music. My Parisian friend stopped and said: 'Sorry, I have to go inside. I am able to resist the temptation of alcohol, cigarettes and even beautiful women, but never the sound of piano music in a bar.'

In this connection, still another significant experience comes to my mind. During those days I had already worked in Paris for fourteen years as a pianist in a little bar and knew a countless number of people, one of whom was an English news reporter who invited me to spend a week in London in order to show me around his beautiful city. On the fourth evening of my visit he had no time to devote to me, because he was obliged to attend a party given by a prominent aristocratic London family. My friend realized that I wouldn't know how to pass the evening alone and suddenly came up with the idea that I should accompany him. He thought it wouldn't be a problem. With the large number of guests attending, the hosts wouldn't be able to tell those who had been invited from those who hadn't.

I threw myself into a rented tuxedo, and my friend pinned a press card to my lapel in order to smuggle me into the party. Once inside, he took the press card away, because the newspaper people all knew each other and would have spotted our ruse.

I sat for several hours between two potted palm trees on a small velvet sofa. From my secluded vantage point I could watch all the prominent figures of London society gathered together. Many of them were internationally known from the press and magazines: personalities of the aristocracy, government ministers, financiers, film stars and Nobel Prize winners. I must confess that I felt very small and unimportant in my little corner and I didn't dare to direct a single word to any of these illustrious people. My friend left me alone for some hours. But finally he appeared accompanied by a lady. As I rose to my feet to be introduced I passed through a moment of panic; the lady was the hostess of the party which I had crashed. I couldn't understand why my friend had taken this risk. And I was even more embarrassed when he said: 'Mr Schott is a piano player in a little bar in Paris.'

At this, I was expecting to be politely escorted to the door by the butler. But the hostess, a perfect lady, smiled. 'Really? ...' she said. 'Oh, I love all those wonderful standards. But most of all I love Gershwin. You couldn't possibly give me greater pleasure than by sitting down at our piano and playing Gershwin.'

She personally led me across the crowded room to a dark Steinway grand piano. I had hardly finished playing some introductory chords to Gershwin's 'Summertime' when people, glasses in hand, began gathering around. Soon the piano was completely surrounded by party guests.

I played Gershwin, Cole Porter, Jerome Kern, Irving Berlin, Hoagy Carmichael, Duke Ellington, Vernon Duke, Richard Rogers and Vincent Youmans. I played all of the beautiful English and Celtic folk songs and the audience enthusiastically sang along with me. I played the whole night through until seven in the morning.

And for years after this memorable evening, I received during each Advent season the most beautiful Christmas card from the gracious hostess and from many of her invited guests, all with personal wishes for my good health and well-being. I don't know which one of all those glittering personalities was supposed to be the centre of attraction that evening. But I'm sure no one expected it to be a piano player from a little bar in Paris.

Playing Popular Music as a Form of Therapy

During my forty years of working as a pianist, I did not of course always work in the same place. I played at Parisian fashion shows, at film parties in Vienna and Munich, at parties held in London by the owners of stables and yachts, as well as in sailors' dives and cabaret bars. I played at the world-famous Parisian 'Harry's New York Bar', frequented by Ernest Hemingway, Jean Paul Sartre, François Sagan, John Steinbeck, William Faulkner and many other famous writers. Now I work only in the bars of large hotels, because I find this kind of work the most pleasant.

During these many years, it has happened again and again that people have paid me a rather strange compliment, which has taken a long time for me fully to understand. They all expressed it slightly differently, but basically they seemed to mean the same thing.

Some people said, for example, 'You know, I suffer so much stress at work, that I just cannot switch off afterwards. I really need to come here for half an hour to listen to you, then I feel okay again.'

Or, another business man explained: 'Your music has an extremely calming effect. I will now go home and sleep unusually well.'

Of course I was not particularly pleased by this comment and gave the man a rather unfriendly look, as he left the bar. Was my playing really so boring that it sent the guests to sleep?

As this guest came to listen to me day after day, for months, I had to assume that I had misunderstood him, and that he was not criticizing my playing. Perhaps he really could only sleep well after my piano playing had released him from the stress of his hectic working day.

A woman broke away from a group of guests who were getting ready to leave the bar, and came over to me at the piano.

'I have such problems at home', she said 'but it's strange, when I listen to you playing the piano my troubles vanish!'

Like this woman, complete strangers tell me their most private problems usually with no preamble, so I often feel like a father confessor. I have listened to problems and given advice. And they came back to report how their situations had developed. I found this satisfying as I could see that they felt relieved and that I had really been able to help them.

This remarkable spontaneous spiritual contact between people can probably be put down to psychic currents which are erased from our sub-consciousness by a certain calming and comforting kind of instrumental music. I cannot help thinking of the Pied Piper, whose confidence-inspiring flute playing caused whole crowds of rats and children to follow him.

Of course as an artist, one is haunted by too many emotions and one's feelings are easily hurt. Now I don't know if, as a humble piano player, I should regard myself as an artist, but it took me a long time to give up a certain sentimental oversensitivity.

I always got rather upset, for example, when people sat around me telling primitive jokes and laughing loudly while I was struggling to give sincere expression to my melodies. I know that as a pianist in a bar one is providing background music rather than giving a recital; people are of course free to choose whether to talk or to listen. But it must be understood that any interpreter of music, to create a certain atmosphere, must summon up a certain means of spiritual communication.

I also found it unpleasant that a well-known French television actor made himself comfortable beside me for a few days. He spread out his papers on the top of the piano and also covered two tables with manuscripts and pages of notes, through which he leafed fervently. One evening he was sitting there with such a furrowed brow and seemed to be in such deep thought about a particularly difficult part of his script, that I tip-toed away from my instrument so as not to disturb him. I went out into the street for half an hour and talked to a young taxi driver, who was studying at the Sorbonne. We talked about astronomy as that evening the Cassiopeia constellation was surprisingly clear over the Paris rooftops, while usually there was only a haze of smog to be seen over our little street. When I finally went back to my instrument, my neighbour kept scowling at me.

'What kept you away for so long?' he hissed. 'You can't just go away and take such a long break!' 'I thought that I was disturbing you', I replied.

'Why should you be disturbing me?' he asked, surprised. 'Why do you think that I am writing my play here then?'

I shrugged my shoulders. 'I don't know', I said, 'perhaps you've got decorators at home.'

'Rubbish! I come here for your music! Do you know what hell it is to have to have a script ready in thirteen days and you just can't think of anything? Complete block, can you understand? A million crazy thoughts whirling around in your mind, all completely useless. You can't sleep, can't think, can't clear out.'

'Clear out?' I wondered.

'Of course … relax, if you can understand that! Clear your mind of the everyday chaos, so that creative thoughts can develop. If you can't keep to your deadlines, you are out of business. Some of us turn to alcohol, some to drugs, and end up on the rubbish heap. For me, piano music such as yours is the best means of release. Look, I have nearly finished my script.'

So I gradually began, over the years, to realize that I am a kind of medical practitioner, helping people to deliver their creative efforts, or a psychiatrist, listening to people's troubles. Nowadays people seem to be bombarded with millions of impulses as a result of ever-increasing technology and pressures of work, that they descend to a state of spiritual tension, from which they cannot escape. It is strange and hard for an outsider to believe – even now I still find it mysterious – that the music of a quietly played piano can have such a calming and relaxing healing effect on stressed people.

Today when I sit down at my piano during the cocktail hour in the hotel bar, and watch the men and women as they flop down into the armchairs around me after a hectic day of work at a fashion show or at a trade fair, I forget that I am a pianist.

During this time I feel more like a psychiatrist, trying to heal spiritual wounds with my music.

I would like to stress that this attitude is not based on arrogance. On the contrary, it is rather a self-reproach! Even after twenty years, I still recall a situation in which my misjudgement might have led to a tragedy.

One of my regular customers, a very pretty, charming and rich young Parisian woman, to my knowledge single, spent nearly every evening in the restaurant in which I was playing at that time because she had been friends with the couple who owned the place since they were children. This lovely girl appeared to be so cheerful that no one would have believed that she suffered from severe depression. Of course I remember that she once requested her favourite song, naming a chanson that was one of the saddest that I have ever played in my life. The song almost gave me goosepimples all over and I couldn't understand why such a lively young girl should want to identify with such dark thoughts.

One evening she put her coat on once again at eleven o'clock and said to me, as always, 'See you tomorrow' at which I told her that I would not be there the next day as I was going on holiday for a fortnight. At that time I was playing at three different places in one evening and often spent time playing sessions during the day at recording studios. I had not had a break for years and felt completely tired and in need of a good break. This might have been why I did not notice her dismay. She stayed for a good fifteen minutes beside the piano, not saying a word, appearing completely disturbed. I thought that perhaps she had had an unpleasant experience and did not for a moment think that her behaviour had anything to do with me as I hardly knew her. But the words that she said to me after her long silence should have warned me.

'Please don't go away on holiday!' she said extremely urgently. 'You don't know how desperately important your music is to me … it is my lifeline! Do you understand?'

Of course I understood nothing and told her about my lack of sleep, that I was completely knocked out and that I just had to have a holiday, or I would fall off my piano stool. At this she just said 'Adieu' and left.

The word 'Adieu' has a certain finality, as if one is not expecting to see someone ever again. When I returned I found out that she was in hospital. She had turned on the gas to take her life; and was only saved by a coincidental telegram messenger who had smelt the gas and had called for help.

I visited her in hospital, where she told me that she had been experiencing a terrible period of unhappiness, which she had been coping with until I had left her in the lurch. For the last year she had found comfort and reassurance in my piano music and, above all the strength to control her depression.

I advised her to begin playing the piano herself ... from memory and in the free way that I did. And to ease my bad conscience and to make amends for my misjudgement, I gave her free lessons for two years. She was very musical, had briefly had classical lessons and applied herself with such enthusiasm and perseverance which verged on obsession. She knew that she finally had an unfailing remedy for her illness. And I was happy to have been able to set an endangered life to rights again in this way.

INTRODUCTION

The Difference Between Reading Music and Playing By Ear

Sitting down at the piano – alone at home, with friends, or at a party – and playing one lovely melody after another, without sheet music, is a fantastic thing. You feel relaxed and everyday cares and worries fade into the distance.

This detached feeling, almost comparable to weightlessness, is unknown to those who are burdened by having to decode symbols on a printed sheet before them. And while they are saddled with this demanding task they cannot relax for an instant, they must constantly maintain a rigid concentration.

Research has shown that playing a musical instrument is more effective in releasing tension than any medication. Playing the piano freely is particularly relaxing. Of course you do not sit down at the piano to protect yourself from the suffering of civilization. You play because you, and hopefully other people too, enjoy it. Freely improvised music reflects the mood of the individual. You can express yourself in major or minor, discreetly or energetically, calmly or with a lively rhythm, depending on how you feel at the time.

This is why you will not find terms like 'hard work', 'tight discipline' or any other such tiresome phrases in the instructions of this book. Our task shall be a kind of leisure-time activity. We will experiment, tinker, give shape and discover sounds in a creative manner. And in this pleasant way we will reach our goal in a relatively short time. All we need to accomplish this objective is genuine interest and a piano or keyboard instrument. But the piano must be in tune because we will be working with the ear. And, also, because the chords of Gershwin and Duke Ellington are more complex and rich in texture than those found in most classical music. They cannot be heard in sharp focus if played on an out-of-tune piano.

Now comes the big question: How can one play the piano without printed music?

17

Letting pearl-like tones flow, improvising freely and going from one song to another? It cannot be done simply through the accident of inherent talent. There must be an underlying method. But which?

Up till now people learning music have always had a railing to support and guide them: notes and symbols printed on a page giving exact information on what to play and how to play it. One cannot take this railing away without offering some other orientation.

We are aiming to master the art of being able to play freely on the piano all the melodies that we know: nursery rhymes, Christmas carols, hymns, folk songs, sea shanties, marches, waltzes, spirituals, country and western songs, blues, jazz, Spanish and South American rhythms, calypso, pop songs, standards, songs from musicals, operettas, and anything else we have ever heard.

If we want to add a new song to our repertoire, we will need only the melody line and the guitar chords.

We also need to be able to play our song a tone higher or lower so that it suits a singer who might like to join in. We should be able to link one song to the next one in a different key. We would like to be able to improvise or, possibly, even compose our own songs. We should also be prepared simply to play an accompaniment as soon as a singer or another instrument takes over the melody; or to play variations when it is our turn to play the melody again. It might happen that some people want to reveal their dancing skills and we are required to play very rhythmically to support the dancers. We may be requested to accompany at a gymnastics or ballet class. There are so many possibilities of playing at home, in schools, clubs or other establishments – alone or with a group of other musicians – once you are able to play the piano freely.

For all these reasons we will now turn to the practical instructions of our first chapter, where we will consider the framework of thought we can construct to enable us to achieve independence from the printed music.

So it remains for me only to wish you great pleasure in your project and also a little perseverance in acquiring the ability to play the piano freely, for your own enjoyment and that of your friends and acquaintances.

CHAPTER 1

WE THRIVE ON CHORDS

Our Chord Display Band

Melody, bass line, accompaniment, variation, improvisation, composition, orchestration and the arpeggio are all nourished by the chord. Even the rhythm sets its clock to the chord. In order to make this clearer I will give an example.

We enter a jazz club where a dixieland band is playing. Against the far wall seven musicians are on a podium with their instruments. We see a piano, drums, tuba, banjo, trombone, trumpet and clarinet in action.

They are in the middle of a piece as we walk in, so we don't immediately recognize it. We don't know that it is 'Oh When the Saints Go Marching In', because none of the crazy musicians feels like playing the melody line. Instead, all seven blow and hammer away wildly without any obvious unifying concept. Each one seems to play the notes that he individually likes, without concern for what the others are doing. But strangely enough, despite this apparent anarchy, it somehow all fits together.

Now, one of them lowers his instrument at a certain point and stops playing altogether. The trombone player who has had his back turned and couldn't even see him, comes in at this split second and takes up the musical thread of his colleague. And the surprising thing is that the trombone player comes from another city. He is working with this band for the first time and has never played this piece with them before. Puzzled, we ask ourselves: By what kind of stopwatch are these musicians working?

21

They don't count, they don't measure, they don't even seem to think about it.

Like a jet pilot flying blind in the fog, they follow their acoustic control beam: ... the chord. Let us use a graphic example in order to make this easier to understand.

Our trombonist, from beginning to the end of the piece, has the camera eye of his subconscious focused on what can be thought of as an auto cue, or chord display band. This band moves from left to right and can be roughly imagined as something like this:

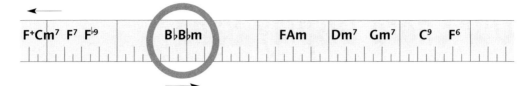

In a split second our imaginary camera-eye aims and focuses and we find ourselves exactly at this point in the song.

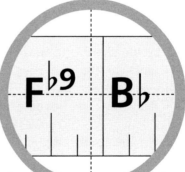

The chord landscape of the moving display band is familiar to the trombone player and his six colleagues down to the smallest detail. Each one knows exactly where he is at any given moment. And what is far more amazing is another function of the moving chord display band: each musician in the group has, with the chord in the focal point of the camera eye, a handful of pre-programmed notes that he can use until the next chord comes into view. These are the four, five or six notes of which the chord is made. And this supply of notes can be doubled by using the same notes in a higher octave.

Consequently, the musician then has eight, ten or even twelve notes at his disposal without the danger of creating disharmony.

All of these notes fit exactly with what the tuba, the banjo, the piano and the rest of the instruments play, because they all come from the same chord shown in the focal point of the sight.

This will also apply if we sit down to the piano one day and improvise a song. We, too, will understand this moving chord display band passing before the camera eye lens of our subconscious, showing every detail of the chord landscape. That is, if we follow through with the instructions to the end of this book and learn how to do this. Our imaginary moving chord display band will constantly guide us and supply us with all the information we need to play the piano by ear.

A chord ...
what's that?

If we examine a scale – a note ladder with eight steps going up and down – we notice that the distance between the third and fourth steps and the seventh and eighth steps is only half the distance as that between the rest of the steps.

This half-step between the third and fourth, and the seventh and eighth steps is the distinguishing characteristic of all major scales. There are twelve of them altogether. (There also exists a second, rarer, type of scale – the minor scale. But we will have less to do with it because it only supplies us with three chords. Later

we will deal with it and it will cause us no difficulty.) At the moment, however, we will concern ouselves only with the major scale; and in particular with the half-step distance between the third and fourth, and the seventh and eighth notes.

Let us now take a major scale, the one which we will most frequently have to deal with, the C major scale. It is called a C major scale simply because it begins on C. Its first step is the note C.

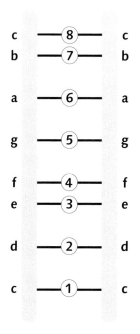

You know the notes C, D, E, F, G, A, B, and C on your piano. From the above diagram you see that the distance between three and four (E - F) and between seven and eight (B - C) are only half-steps. This is also true on our piano; because between all the other keys there is also a black one, but not between E and F, and B and C.

Our piano is known to be divided into half tones, also know as semitones. When we go from key to key, ascending step by step, whether or not it is a black or white key that comes first in the rising order, we always climb upwards by semitone steps.

The following illustration of our piano keys comprising the C major scale readily demonstrates that the notes C, D, E, F, G, A, B, C must be a major scale because of the semitone step between E - F and B - C. All of the other notes in the scale have a distance of a whole tone between them.

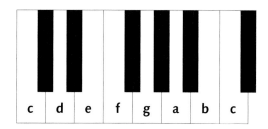

I explain all of this in such detail, because the names, components and functions of chords will only remain an eternal mystery to those who have never been told that chords are born from scales.

As you can see from the note ladder there are actually only seven instead of eight steps, because the eighth step brings us once again to C. And with that C the ladder to the next floor begins.

Striking all seven piano keys of the C major scale at the same time will produce a terrible discord, because some of the notes do not go along with each other. But certain ones selected from the scale harmonize wonderfully with each other. If we now find out some notes which harmonize together, producing a pleasing sensation to the ear, we will have a chord. A chord is a structure of three or more harmonizing notes.

Working with eleven chord-types

All eleven basic chords which originate from the C major scale or from the C minor scale (eight major chords and three minor chords) carry the family name of C. Only their first names are different.

C

The first of our eleven chords has no first name. It is simply called C. We can consider it as the head of the family of all the C chords. If one would speak of the head of the Bloomfield family one certainly wouldn't bother using the first name, but would simply refer to him as 'the Old Bloomfield'.

Suppose that you get invited to a party where you only know the hosts. You are introduced to many people and hear a number of names which you try to remember. But after half an hour you find you can't remember a single one any more.

A week later you meet the host, seated with a gentleman, in a cafe and he says to you: 'You already know my friend Bloomfield. I introduced you to him at the party.'

You think: 'Aha! this gentleman is called Bloomfield. He is short, red-haired, has a round face with a walrus moustache, and wears metal-rimmed glasses.'

The next time you meet him you will certainly remember his name immediately, without the slightest difficulty.

Our eleven chords also have their own proper names and typical identifying characteristics. And with them it is much easier, because the name of each chord immediately gives us precise information about his looks.

This leading chord consists of those three notes of the C major scale which fit best together, namely the basic pillars of the scale, *c* - *e* - *g*.

To avoid confusion, we will write all the note names in small ***italic*** letters and the chord symbols in capital letters from now on.

It possesses only three notes and is called a triad; whereas the remaining ten chords of the family have four or even five notes. So if we now see the C on our moving chord display band, we will automatically know that we have to work with the three notes *c* - *e* - *g*. But as a matter of fact this symbol C does not prescribe how or how often we have to use these notes; nor in which octave we should play them on the piano. Just like our dixieland musicians we can play *c* - *e* - *g* in any order or combination, singly or all at once, doubled or tripled – anything goes.

The C on our moving chord display band says only that in the accompaniment of our song, in some manner or order, we must use the notes *c* - *e* - *g* and no others. And to continue doing so until the next chord appears in the focus of our camera eye lens.

The variety of possibilities given to us by the musical symbol C is at first confusing. How and where shall we strike these three notes? And what do we play in the bass?

Relax, there's nothing to worry about. We will begin by keeping to one definite

pattern which will make things clear and easy. In the right hand we will use only three different combinations for the C chord:

With the left hand, we play a low *c* in the bass. Together it looks like this:

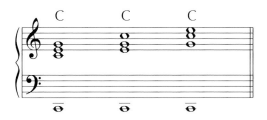

We will now take an example using the following melody line with the chord symbol C over the staff:

Here we did not repeat the C symbol over each note as we did in the preceding example. It is sufficient to place it over the first note of the series to be accompanied by *c* - *e* - *g*. And we continue

this accompaniment with the melody line until a new chord symbol appears.

With the symbol C we now know quite clearly how to form the accompaniment to this melody:

In case you wish to play the accompaniment faster, but find it difficult to strike the chord with each note of the melody line, you can do the following:

Of course, you can also play the **c** in the bass more often. Instead of playing only semibreves (whole notes) you can use minims (half notes), or even crotchets (quarter notes) if you wish. The symbol C leaves you with several possibilities. But nevertheless, you have a firm concept to work with.

I readily admit that what we are playing here must sound extremely simple and primitive to your ear, but we are still at the beginning. I only want to introduce you to the eleven chords of the C family, in this first chapter. Later, we will concern ourselves with how to work with them in detail.

Here we have our next party guest. He is called C[6] ('C-six'). C is the family name and the high-placed [6] is his first name.

The C says, once again, that the chord stands on the basic ground **c - e - g**. The high-placed [6] shows that we add another note from the C major scale: The note of the sixth step.

Whether we like it or not, there is no other possibility given to us; the chord must look like this:

The building blocks that make up this chord are called **c - e - g - a**. As a matter of fact, these notes can also be inverted and placed at different pitch-levels:

Each one of these chords is still C^6; because no matter in which position the notes are arranged, the same building blocks are being used, *c - e - g - a*. Now, in order to get a better grasp of the four possibilities of this chord, play them a few times with the right hand to get them firmly under the fingers.

From now on, the C^6 will never again be a stranger to us no matter in which guise we see him later on. As in the case of our short, red-haired Mr Bloomfield with the walrus moustache, we will recognize him and greet him by name wherever we meet him; no matter if we find him dressed in white tie and tails on his way to the theatre, or surprise him at home in a jogging suit doing yoga exercises. He will always be the same Mr Bloomfield.

Similarly, should the C^6 appear on our moving chord display band, we will know we have to use the notes *c - e - g - a* in accompanying the melody, and no others! In the bass we will take a low *c* which we can change once in a while to a higher octave if we wish.

The melody line with which we will be practising now already has two chord symbols: C and C^6. Therefore we can apply the following combinations for our accompaniment.

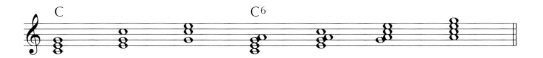

Actually, we have additional possibilities for our right hand, because it may happen that the melody moves higher or lower. In that case we should play our accompanying chord one octave higher or lower. We will try now to fit the following designated chords to the given melody line.

Take your time in picking up the required chords. Have a look at the line with the seven possible chord combinations on this page. Take it easy, and play the melody very, very slowly to get used to changing back and forth between C and C^6. Here is the written-out voicing with the bass:

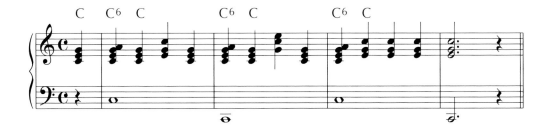

Now, I will give you a second example of a melody where the C[6] appears in other positions, in order to establish its specific sound in your ear. At one place the melody goes down, so we must play one of the C combinations an octave lower.

And here once again are the written-out piano voices with the bass. There is no chord symbol over the first two notes of the melody, so we play them alone, without chord or bass accompaniment.

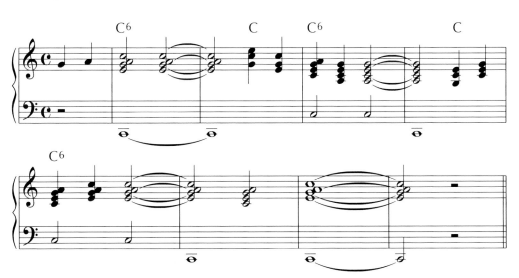

I think that is sufficient for the first presentation of the C[6]. If it reappears in our moving chord display band, we will know exactly what it is and how to deal with it. Let us now turn to our next chord.

Distinguished people do not allow themselves to be commanded as ordinary people do. It is rather embarrassing for them to receive orders such as: 'Now, do a handstand!' or: 'Lie down on the carpet!'

Here we encounter an elegant member of the C family, distinguished and reserved, with a discreet, uncommon sound. This chord must take on a second abbreviated first name, because its impertinent cousin already calls himself C⁷, although not entitled to that term.

Since our distinguished friend is a half head higher than his cheeky cousin, he put the letter 'j' before his first name (7), which means major.

At the moment, however, we won't concern ourselves with this family squabble over first names. We know that our Cj⁷ belongs to the main branch of the C family; that he is legally entitled to this first name 7, and is therefore composed of four notes which you can easily guess – the basic notes **c - e - g**, plus the 7th note of the C major scale, namely the **b**.

In just the same way, our Cj⁷ is very reluctant to be commanded to other positions. And whenever he has to perform this necessity, under no circumstances does he do it without his butler – the bass.

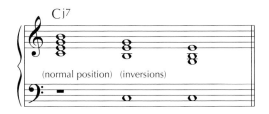

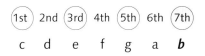

So it has to look like this, written on the staff:

Even if the Cj⁷ is unknown in folk songs, it is a very important creative element in blues, jazz, bossa novas, melodies from musicals and standards. So let us now see a melody line with chords we already know, and with the Cj⁷ in addition.

On the piano we should then play the above line like this:

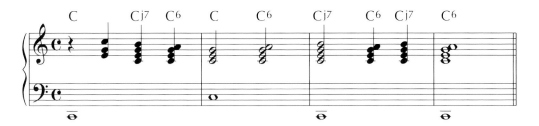

Of course, it should be clear to us that with the three chords we now possess, we cannot give shape to a complete song yet. And continuously playing *c* in the bass is absolutely dull and boring. But as I have already stated, this first chapter only deals with the presentation of the eleven basic chords of the C family. The same eleven chord types exist in other note families. But this need not cause you alarm. By the end of this chapter it will be child's play for you to make use of the same eleven basic chords in the note families F or G, for example.

Now let us take a look at a melody line consisting of one single note, but using the three different chords we have learned.

According to the system we are following our accompaniment will look like this:

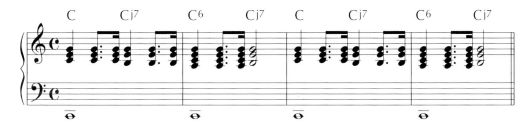

One occasionally finds this chord sequence as an introduction to a song, or as a transition from one part to another, whereby the C or the C^6 in the right hand is often left out.

As a matter of fact, one can leave out one or other of the notes with most chords. But it is not allowed to substitute a note in the chord which does not belong there, without it being indicated by the chord symbol.

Now, we will make the acquaintance of another member of the C family. It is in fact the twin brother of the C^{j7}, equally distinguished and reserved.

Here, it could be asked: How can a chord acquire a '9' when there are only seven notes in the scale. The answer is that we continue the scale up into the next floor.

(1st)	2nd	(3rd)	4th	(5th)	6th	7th	8th	(9th)
c	d	e	f	g	a	b	c	**d**

As a matter of fact, the ninth note has the same name and the same characteristic sound as the second note – **d**. Only, it is located an octave higher. Now if a chord symbol requires an additional **d** to the basic pillars **c** - **e** - **g**, one can hardly take the second step of the scale, because,

situated between the **c** and the **e**, it would sound discordant. Therefore one uses the higher **d**, the one on the ninth step, which gives a more pleasant sound.

We have to take into account that the C^{j9} is the twin brother of our C^{j7}; practically a second, extended version, a chord which has a little hat on … the nine. This has the consequence that the C^{j9} has to be played as an added ninth to the C^{j7}. The seventh step of this chord is always included although it is not mentioned in the chord symbol C^{j9}. Therefore instead of four notes, the C^{j9} has five: The three basic notes of the scale, **c** - **e** - **g**, as well as the seventh step, **b**, and the ninth, **d**.

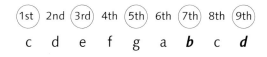

(1st)	2nd	(3rd)	4th	(5th)	6th	(7th)	8th	(9th)
c	d	e	f	g	a	**b**	c	**d**

Such a chord is not easy to play with the right hand alone. Consequently we play the note **c** with the left hand in the bass, and the remaining four notes with the right hand

C^{j9} is even more headstrong than his twin brother C^{j7}. He doesn't like to be bossed around at all, and you rarely find him in other positions.

Let us now take a melody line in which the C^{j9} occurs.

Slowly

C C⁶ Cʲ⁷ Cʲ⁹ C C⁶ Cʲ⁷ C⁶

The chord symbols tell us what we have to play with the melody line. We can place the **c** in the bass wherever we wish.

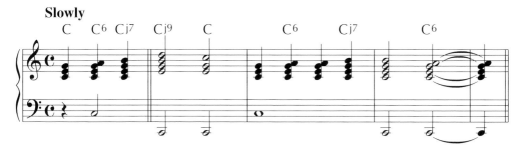

Slowly

C C⁶ Cʲ⁷ Cʲ⁹ C C⁶ Cʲ⁷ C⁶

With jazz ballads and other forms of modern music with a slower tempo, the Cʲ⁷ will occasionally appear as the final chord. For instance it might be used as shown in the example below.

We have now learned four of the eleven chord types. And we can build without any difficulty the C, the C⁶, the Cʲ⁷ and the Cʲ⁹ if these chord symbols appear on our moving chord display band.

As I have already mentioned before, the same chord types occur not only in C, but in all of the other note families as well. If we now see on our moving chord display band an F⁶ from the note family F, for example, then we know that this chord is from the F major scale and not from the C major scale.

F major scale:

f	g	a	bflat	c	d	e	f	g
1st	2nd	3rd	4th	5th	6th	7th	8th	9th

The 3 basic pillars + ⁶th step = F⁶

The F⁶ comes from the three basic notes of the F major scale, *f - a - c*, and the sixth note, *d*, of this scale: *f - a - c - d*.

You see, there really is nothing to it, once we have understood the construction of the basic chords. But let us return to our C major family on which we are concentrating in this first chapter.

With the C, C^6, C^{j7} and C^{j9} we now have all the members of the main line of the C family. Next, we will meet four chords, ones which develop along secondary lines: … cousins with a dash of foreign blood in their veins, i.e. chords which must borrow one of their notes from a foreign scale.

Here we have the cheeky cousin who insists upon being called C^7. As the 7 is not available to him in the C major scale, he simply steals a similar note from another scale and boldly calls himself C^7, whether it is related or not.

The stolen note is the *b flat* of the F major scale, a note that obviously does not belong to the family of C major. C^7 consists therefore of the three basic pillars *c - e - g* with the added *b flat* from the F family.

It is quite scandalous: although our C^7 is thus clearly exposed as a trickster, he enjoys – perhaps especially because of his cheeky appearance – tremendous popularity. He is a big shot amongst chords, the most celebrated chord in classical music as well as operetta, in folk music and songs of all kinds, in the waltz, in the march, in church music and, as far as I know, in all other kinds. He is inundated with praise, school harmony books bestow on him the grandiose title of dominant seventh … and all that for a little fraud and pick-pocket!

You have to acknowledge, however, that he has great charm and tremendous powers of attraction, which is often the case with fraudsters. Through his close relationship with the F family he is in the position to relate any chord that precedes him to the F family. As soon as he appears somewhere, he dominates and pushes the sounds in the direction of F major even though they did not originally want to go there. That can sometimes be very over-powering; but strangely enough nobody minds.

In this chapter, as we are not yet dealing with F major – although C^7 leads all other chords directly to F chords – I cannot show you any melody lines at the moment in which C^7 appears as it would immediately lead us to unfamiliar territory.

In the meantime let us instead look at the positions in which he may be found. This C^7 is not as distinguished and reticent as his cousin C^{j7}. He is loud and pushy, always wants to be the centre of attention and sets out to be a talking point. This is why he allows himself to be admired, reproduced and distributed in all positions.

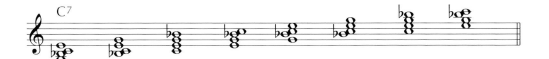

Anyway, it will not do any harm if you take the trouble to play the C^7 inversions frequently so that you get to know them well. Leaping quickly from one pitch-range to another is by no means easy. It must be clear in our minds that, for example, in folk tunes in F major, we will encounter C^7 on almost every second chord.

It is different in jazz music. There, C^7 in its pure form is considered rather primitive and boring and musicians try to disguise or avoid it wherever possible. It is often replaced with C^9.

Just like C^{j7}, C^7 also has a twin brother, a second, extended version which has the ninth added like a kind of little hat. This ninth is the regular **d** from the C major scale, i.e. the same note that is added to

the C^{j9}. The difference between C^{j9} cnd C^9 is only that the C^{j9} has the real seventh, **b**, while the C^9 has to use the **b flat** from the F major scale stolen by his smart twin brother.

So that we do not create any confusion here, we will show the four chords in root position next to each other:

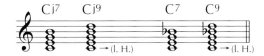

You can see that the C^9 consists of the building blocks of the C^7, so that this chord also always includes the (false) seventh although it is not included in the chord symbol. So the seventh should not be excluded here. Just like the C^{j9}, the C^9 consists of five notes and we must play the **c** with the left hand.

If you compare the C^{j7} with the C^7 in the above musical example, you will see that the distinguished C^{j7} is in fact half a tone higher than his cheeky cousin and that his second name, abbreviated with 'j', is quite rightly 'major = greater'.

As we will frequently use C^9 in sophisticated standards and in jazz, we will take a look at the four positions straight away. In the musical example there are six, but the last two inversions are the same as the first two only one octave higher.

C^9

In principle, C^9 is not nearly as complicated as it may appear in notated form: if we add a **d** somewhere to a C^7 chord – no matter which position it is in – we have a C^9. And that is all we need to know about C^9 for the time being.

Here we have a chord of the C family that at first looks rather mysterious. In reality he is a harmless chap.

The C means that this chord consists of the three basic pillars **c - e - g** of the C major scale. The plus sign indicates that the highest note of these three basic pillars, i.e. the **g**, is raised by a semitone. That is all.

C+

In many countries the chord symbol C^{5+} is used, which shows more clearly that the fifth step of the C major scale, the **g**, should be raised by a semitone.

So this chord too has had to borrow one of its notes from another scale, as **g sharp** does not appear in the C major scale. C+ is no fraudster, however, as his symbol clearly indicates that he has borrowed a note from a foreign scale.

You have no doubt heard this chord with its rather strange sound. It is the final chord of a tango. Actually it should be followed by another chord, but that is omitted in the real Argentinian tango.

We will look at this more closely in later chapters. At the moment we are concerned only with the position in which it usually appears. Sometimes it is even mixed a little with C^7. That is, the false 7 of the C^7, i.e. the **b flat**, is added. The chord symbol indicates this as follows:

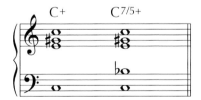

C+ $C^{7/5+}$

It should also be added that C+, even when it is not mixed with C^7, still has the same relationship with the F chords as the C^7. So I will not yet introduce melody lines in which the C+ appears.

As the last member of the C major family, I must introduce a poor relative of distant lineage. He inherited only a **c** and an **a** from the C major scale and was forced to beg for two notes from foreign scales in order to continue existing. Of course he shows this honestly on his flag, although you have to look at his résumé in a little detail otherwise you will not learn much from the little ring, or zero, or whatever it is, that appears in his name.

This C° did not want to remain a poor relative. He wanted to get somewhere. So with his two acquired notes he tried his hand at competitive sport and invented a new discipline – four-jump – in which he immediately became a champion. Beginning on low **c**, it involves jumping over two half tones four times and landing exactly on **c** of the next octave. There you can continue and in this way jump through the next octave as well.

So you hop from **c** to **e flat**, from **e flat** to **g flat**, from **g flat** to **a**, from **a** to **c**, from **c** to **e flat** of the next octave and so on up to the highest notes: … a never-ending cycle, a cat that chases its own tail. That is what the little circle of his banner is trying to indicate.

Let us compare on the keyboard the intervals of the C° chord with those of the three basic pillars of the C major chord – i.e. those of the very first chord with which we became acquainted. We can see that the interval between the three pillars is not equal: **c** and **e** are further apart than **e** and **g**.

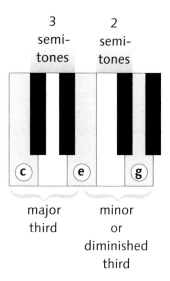

In fact there are three semitones between the first and second pillars, whereas there are only two between the second and third. The first interval is therefore called a major third. The second interval is called a minor third or a diminished third.

A minor third is thus an interval with two semitone steps in between, i.e. exactly the type of interval that creates the perpetual movement of our C°. This chord may also be given the indication C^{dim}; dim being the abbreviation of 'diminished'.

Here is another short musical example, from which you will see that our poor relative of the C major family, with its leaping abilities, has possibly achieved the most outlandish sound quality of the whole family. Anyway, you have to admit that our chords do not by any means sound as primitive as at the beginning of the chapter. C° is in any case a welcome guest of all composers, from Bach to Duke Ellington. It is a very important element, without which music would be much the poorer.

With C° we have now become acquainted with the eight chords of the C major family, that is, chords that take their building blocks from the C major scale: C, C^6, C^{j7}, C^{j9}, C^7, C^9, C$^+$ and C°. We have only to get to know the three chords of the C minor family, mentioned at the beginning, i.e. the three chords that take their building blocks from the C minor scale.

Then we will have met all of our party guests. All eleven types of chords will then be familiar to us and we will be able to proceed with renewed confidence, working with them and we can select them from our range of chords whenever we require them.

Let's now turn to our C minor family, from which our three missing chords come. This is quite a different breed: soft, melancholy types with drooping moustaches and sad eyes. There are no airheads and imposters such as our C^7 amongst them, and not one of them would break away from his funeral march to perform such risky leaps as our C°.

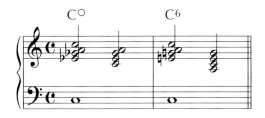

This is the ancestor of the C minor family. He too consists of only three notes: the three supporting pillars of the scale of C minor. These three supporting pillars are not *c* - *e* - *g*, as in the major scale, but *c* - *e flat* - *g*. So there is a slight difference. Let's write down the C major chord beside the C minor chord:

It should not be difficult to recognize the three different inversions of the C minor chord:

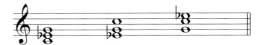

If we compare the first five steps of a major scale with those of a minor scale, then we see a slight difference, which is that in the minor scale the famous semitone step appears between the second and third steps, differing from the major scale, where the semitone appears between the third and fourth steps.

Minor			Major		
g	5	g	g	5	g
f	4	f	f	4	f
			e	3	e
e flat	3	e flat			
d	2	d	d	2	d
c	1	c	c	1	c

As a result of this, the distances between the three supporting pillars are of course changed slightly. In the major chord we have the major third at the bottom and the minor third at the top. In the minor chord the minor third is at the bottom and the major third is at the top. That is the only difference!

An even simpler explanation is: in the minor scale the third step is a semitone lower than in the major scale.

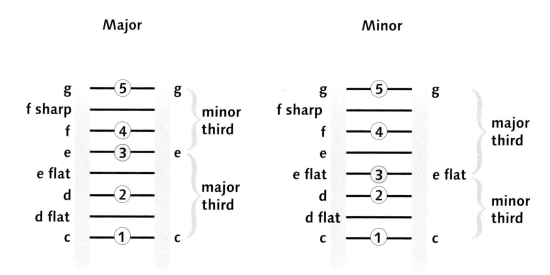

Major — **Minor**

That is all we need to know about C minor for the time being.

Even Cm[6] and the remaining Cm[7] would theoretically be very simple to produce if there was just one minor scale. Unfortunately there are three kinds of minor scales in competition with each other!

Thankfully at least the five lower steps are the same in all three. So we don't have any problems here. Only the sixth and seventh steps are different in the three minor scales.

There is the aeolian (pure) minor scale, which comes from mediaeval church music. Then there is the harmonic minor scale. And the third kind is the melodic minor scale, in which the sixth and seventh steps differ ascending and descending.

Aeolian (pure) minor scale:

6th step 7th step   7th step 6th step

Harmonic minor scale:

6th step 7th step   7th step 6th step

Melodic minor scale:

6th step 7th step   7th step 6th step (different descending)

Although any Gipsy violinist, even from the most remote little village, must play these three minor scales, up and down, for a lifetime – to win the hearts of his pretty little piroschkas, we do not need to concern ouselves too much with them.

The fact that these minor scales appear so complicated and create such a fuss because of their 6th and 7th steps does actually give us a great advantage as we can choose from the different sixth and seventh steps whichever sounds best with the minor triad. For Cm^6 we take the sixth step (the **a**) from the ascending melodic minor scale. It goes extremely well with the C minor triad.

It also sounds really good in the three other inversions:

When you play these minor chords on the piano you can clearly hear their melancholy character. This applies to Cm, Cm^6 and Cm^7.

41

Cm7

The seventh step for the Cm^7 is taken from the descending melodic minor scale. This **b flat** is also used for the seventh step of the aeolian minor scale as it goes very well with the minor sound. So our Cm^7 consists of: **c - e flat - g - b flat**.

Later we will see this Cm^7 appearing frequently on our moving chord display band. In many chord progressions it takes on the function of a herald, preparing the way, which I will talk about in more depth later on. For the time being I would like to show you a short melody with our three minor chords:

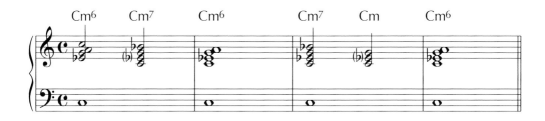

With such chords you have to be careful not to become depressed. If you want to compose a funeral march that will have you and your audience in floods of tears, you only have to select these chords.

With these last three gloomy party guests our introduction ceremony is now complete. It is of course not enough to know someone's name. From now on, however, we will meet these eleven chord-types again and again. We will work with them and get to know them so well that we will soon come across their little secrets, and their different characteristics and tendencies will be revealed to us.

CHAPTER 2

VISIT FROM THE NEIGHBOURHOOD

We earth-dwellers live on the third planet – named Terra by the Romans – of our solar system. Our sun is situated in one of the outer spirals of the Milky Way galaxy; to be more precise on the inner edge of Orion's Belt which, like all branches of the Milky Way, with its convex side leading the way, spins out of the spiral like a fire wheel.

With this brief look at our solar system, I would just like to bring to mind the greatness of the universe to which we belong, and emphasize what a tiny part of this our earth is. A tragic fixation on petty issues has led the human race to a dead-end situation of conflict and war, from which it will never be free. How could the inhabitants of this small, insignificant planet come closer together, when after 2,000 years of 'culture', we are still trying to communicate with over 10,000 languages and over 100,000 dialects. Apart from the few dozen expressions that are used internationally, from the many thousand subjects of interest, only mathematics and music have managed to evolve a system that can be understood by people from all over the world. This achievement is not to be underestimated.

Music is really the only universal language. Just like our notation system, chord symbols can be understood by pop and jazz musicians from all over the world. The jazz trumpeter in New Orleans works from our chord symbols, as does a bossa-nova guitarist in Rio, a Hawaiian ukulele player, a Grand Hotel dance band, helping the rich people of Alaska to forget the cold polar nights, or the ragtime pianist on a hotel terrace illuminated by tropical stars somewhere in Senegal. These symbols are used even in Ceylon or Borneo, in Manila, Toyko, Australia or New Zealand.

Of course there are slight differences here and there in the symbols used. But any insider will be aware of these. We have already seen that our $C°$ is sometimes given as C^{dim} (diminished). Instead of C^+, C^{5+} might be indicated, as we have heard. Or you might also find C^{+5}. Occasionally you might also see the symbol C^{5aug} or C^{aug}, i.e. the abbreviation for augmented (raised).

Instead of C^{j7} or C^{j9} you will often find the extended indications C^{maj7} or C^{maj9}. This will not present you with any problems as you already know that this is a major chord. Composers and arrangers are sometimes rather brief with their chord indications and write simply Cj, leaving it to the individual whether to play a C^{j7} or C^{j9}.

Minor chords may be indicated as Cmin, $Cmin^6$ and $Cmin^7$.

Here is a list of all the variations:

C						
C^6						
C^{j7}	=	C^{maj7}	=	C^j		
C^{j9}	=	C^{maj9}	=	C^j		
C^7						
C^9						
C^+	=	C^{5+}	=	C^{+5}	=	C^{5aug}
$C°$	=	C^{dim}				
Cm	=	Cmin				
Cm^6	=	$Cmin^6$				
Cm^7	=	$Cmin^7$				

There is also another variant of C^9, which we will come to later. To improve its sound a slight alteration is sometimes made to this chord. It sounds rather good if you lower the ninth step by a semitone. Of course this must be shown in the chord symbol: either as C^{b9}, or as C^{9-}. The *d* (the ninth) then becomes *d flat*. This variant of C^9 is found only in a certain inversion. We will take a closer look at C^9, as using this chord will give your playing an interesting touch.

I have already mentioned that no notes should be added to the basic chord construction indicated by the symbol. It is different though when the symbol indicates that an additional note is required. We have already seen such an example with C^+, to which the seven of the C^7 is sometimes added, which is then indicated in the chord symbol as $C^{7/5+}$ or simply $C^{7/+}$. Let's take a look once again at the notation in this case, which we encountered earlier.

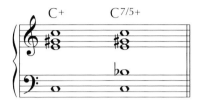

So here a foreign note should be added to a particular chord. There are two such extra notes that can be added to C^7: $C^{7/4}$ and $C^{7/6}$. You will probably have already realized that this means you add the 4th or 6th step of the C major scale to C^7.

Occasionally you will find instead of $C^{7/4}$ a rather unclear symbol infiltrating our mathematical figuration system. You will then see C^{7sus4}. The indication 'sus4' or simply 'sus' is the abbreviation for 'suspended 4'. Instead of the 3rd step belonging to the chord (*e*) the fourth step (*f*) is 'suspended'. This chord has a certain tension, you can hear that the 4th step wants to 'resolve' on to the 3rd step.

With $C^{7/4}$ you know at a glance that a C^7 is required with the fourth step of the scale of C major (*f*) instead of the third step. Our system sets everything down very clearly. Even if you occasionally come across a symbol that you haven't seen before, with your existing knowledge of chords, you will be able to work out what is meant, for example:

$$C^{9-/5+}$$

$$Cm^{7/5-}$$

$$Cm^{7/4}$$

$C^{9-/5+}$ can only mean that the 9 is lowered by a semitone and that the 5 is raised by a semitone.

$Cm^{7/5-}$ is a Cm^7 in which the 5th step is lowered by a semitone.

And with $Cm^{7/4}$ the Cm^7 chord has the 4th step of the C minor scale (*f*) instead of the 3rd.

There is another thing I should perhaps mention here. You will often see the word 'tacet' or 'guitar tacet' written between the chord symbols. Tacet is a Latin term meaning 'be silent'. At the section of a song marked tacet, only the melody is played: there is no chordal accompaniment.

In a band, of course, it is not only the piano that should be silent, but also the backing guitar. That is what is meant by 'guitar tacet'. Sometimes you might see the abbreviation n.c., which means 'no chord'.

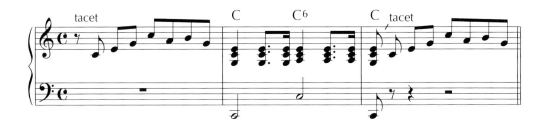

I hope that this rather detailed look at the subject of chord symbols has not been too confusing. The aim was to present the eleven chord-types and to explain the system of figuration to you.

In the following part of the book we will apply this knowledge in practice. If something still puzzles you, there are plenty of examples to come that will help clarify matters. In addition, at the end of the book you will find several tables giving an overview of all the chords in every possible inversion, which will certainly answer some of your questions.

Perhaps you wondered about the title of this second chapter, which reads 'Visit From the Neighbourhood'. Of course we are not talking about the arrival of the inhabitants of another planet belonging to our solar system, but simply becoming acquainted with chords that were unfamiliar to us as they are not related to members of the C family.

Here it is extremely important to keep clearly in mind that all eleven chords of the C family are based on components of the C major or C minor scale, and that both of these scales are called C scales because their first and most important note – their key note – is *c*. All eleven chords of the C family are based on this keynote.

In music, however, there is not only the note *c*, but also eleven other notes (*c sharp*, *d*, *d sharp*, *e*, *f*, *f sharp*, *g*, *g sharp*, *a*, *b flat* and *b*). Of course each of these eleven notes is also the key note of a major or minor scale. Whether we look at the scale of E major/E minor or the scale of G major/G minor, or any other of the 12 existing major or minor scales: each one has eleven chord-types based on its own personal scale components. So, just like in the C family, the E family consists of: E, E^6, E^{j7}, E^7, E^9, E^+, $E°$, Em, Em^6 and Em^7. The chords based on G are: G, G^6, G^{j7}, G^{j9}, G^7, G^9, G^+, $G°$, Gm, Gm^6 and Gm^7.

If you add them all up, you will find that there are 12 major/minor scales and each major/minor combination produces 11 chords. So altogether there are 132 chords.

Do not be alarmed! Apart from the members of the C family, which are already familiar to us, we need only concern ourselves with two dozen foreign visitors at the most. And they will not appear all at once. Some of them appear here and there and some are very rarely seen. So there is no need to panic.

Besides, you are now already in a position to read any unfamiliar chord from a lead sheet and to construct it immediately.

What would happen, for example, if you came across an F^6? You simply take the 1st, 3rd and 5th notes of the F major scale (*f*, *a*, *c*) and add the 6th step (i.e. the *d*). And this is exactly how you proceed with the other unfamiliar chords from any other groups of scales. The basic chord always consists of the 1st, 3rd and 5th steps of the appropriate scale. If another note from the scale is required in addition, you will see this from the figures given.

To begin with we shall not make our work over-complicated and will first play our melodies in C major. This means that we shall concern ourselves with the eleven chords we already know of the C family and add a few visitors from the neighbourhood to bring a bit more colour into our chord playing.

Anyone who plays standards and popular tunes for years will soon realize that on the whole the same chord combinations appear again and again. It is a bit like a box of toy building bricks. In certain places the same blocks are found together. In musical terms we speak of 'sequences'. At a certain point in a song, if you hear two chords in succession, you can often tell in advance what the third chord will be.

This practice is quite common nowadays in technology. Televisions are not built as they used to be, when all the necessary parts were installed individually in the casing. Today certain parts are mounted together in a group, which is called a module. Modules are thus units consisting of several individual parts assembled together that may be installed in certain places or exchanged as required.

From now on we shall proceed according to this system, assembling those chords that almost always appear in the same order into small, interchangeable units. We shall find out at which place of a melody one chord module or another best fits in … an interesting construction project.

I don't know if you have noticed; until now, in all our musical examples, the notes of the melody were also the upper notes of the chord.

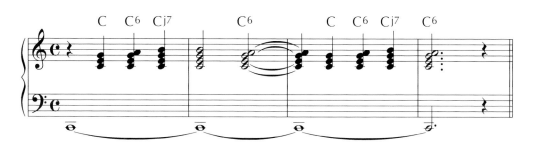

49

The notes of the melody were added to the chord symbol. For instance, you will see in the last musical example that in the second chord the **a** of the melody is added to the chord symbol, as the chord is indicated as C^6 and the 6 is simply the **a** of the melody.

This can be the case, but it need not be so. In general the melody is an independent part of a song, as the bass and the chords are individual musical elements, even though they all fit together harmonically.

The melody is thus a self-sufficient part of the music and does not belong to the accompanying chord. *It does not have to be mentioned in the symbol.* It will be played whether there is a chord beneath it or not.

In other words, we could have simply given the symbol C for the second chord of the last musical example, instead of C^6. Even the C^{j7} chords that appear in this example could have been notated simply as C as the j^7 step – the **b** – appears in the melody and therefore does not need to be mentioned in the chord symbol. So, for the whole system, a single C would have sufficed.

There is an even better reason why the melodic notes should be regarded as independent. It often happens that a chord is indicated beneath a melodic note, in which the melodic note does not appear at all. That sounds rather complicated, but it is not difficult to explain. Let's look at the C° (C diminished), for example.

You can place this chord beneath the melodic notes **b** or **d** and these combinations sound very good, although neither **b** or **d** have anything to do with this chord.

So, this C° goes very well beneath a melodic passage that ascends in steps from **d** to **a**. It should not concern us that the first three times this chord is played – without the melody – there are only three instead of all four notes, as the **a** is missing. We know that not all of the chords of a given symbol need to be used. You are quite free to leave out one of them. You may not, however, play a note that does not belong to the chord (unless it is a melodic note), unless it is added to the symbol.

Likewise, we can distribute the notes freely, at different pitches. This descending melody, for example, sounds much better if, instead of using the key note **c** of the chord, you use the **e flat** in the bass.

More often in standards, you will find that this 4-note descending melody is harmonized with two different chords. That is, the first two notes with C and the second two with C°. Here, too, we will use the third of the chord in the bass rather than the key note. The whole thing will look like this:

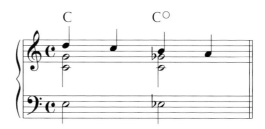

And there we have our first module, a unit that consists of two chords linked together, which we can always use with this typical step-wise descending melodic sequence. It can also be used in many other places.

This descending melodic pattern, from the 9th to the 6th step, that often appears in standards, can be found with many different rhythmic variations. It may look like this in one song:

or like this:

51

Or, somewhere in France, you might hear a Valse Musette that goes like this:

But, whatever rhythmic attire this melodic sequence may wear, he will always accompany it with the chord-module C - C°.

So, now I will show you which chord-module you can use when this step-wise descending melodic line continues for another four steps, that is, when the melody looks like this:

We already know how to harmonize the first bar: C - C°. For the accompaniment to the second bar, we borrow two visitors from the neighbourhood: Dm^7 and G^9 (G^7 with a little hat).

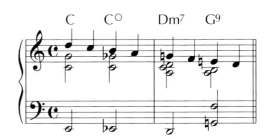

The two visitors from the neighbourhood in the second bar of the previous musical example are so important and appear so often that we have dedicated a whole chapter to this module (Dm^7 - G^9).

CHAPTER 3

THE GREAT IMPRESARIO AND HIS HERALD

The so-called seventh chords (C^7, G^7, D^7, etc.) are the great impresarios on the music scene. In the first chapter, in which C^7 (the cheeky cousin of C^{j7}) was introduced, we heard that this member of the C family is so popular that he is always appearing somewhere and he is always calling the tune. Furthermore, we found out about C^7, that with his false seventh (**b flat**) – borrowed from the scale of F major, – he pulls the chord progression in the direction of F major.

The other seventh chords, G^7, D^7, A^7, etc., of course also have this effect. They too force the accompaniment away from the components of the original scale and towards the chord whose key note lies four notes higher. G^7, with whom we now concern ourselves, could actually be counted as a member of the C family because all of its notes (**g**, **b**, **d**, **f**) appear in the scale of C major. So whether it appears purely as G^7 or as a variant (G^9, $G^{7/+}$, etc.), he pulls us towards the C chords.

I admit, this is no amazing discovery. Most of you will have known this for a long time. But I must mention it as we are dealing with the Dm^7 - G^7 module. After G^7 has led to C, we can immediately add a third component, i.e. C. So in the end our module looks like this: Dm^7 - G^7 - C. This is the most commonly used fixed chord-module.

Now you might ask what the Dm^7 is doing here. He has nothing to do with C major. Or does he? ... At first glance, perhaps not, but if we look closer we can establish that all four notes – **d**, **f**, **a**, **c**, do not only appear in the scale of D minor, but they also appear in the scale of C major. So D minor, just like G^7, is really no stranger

to the C family. Thus in the whole module Dm^7 - G^7 - C there are no foreign notes, i.e. they all belong to the C major scale.

Dm^7 consists of the basic chord of the scale of D minor, that is, the 1st, 3rd and 5th steps of this scale: *d*, *f*, *a*. In addition to this comes the 7th step given in the symbol, the *c*.

These four notes can then appear in different inversions:

In simple folk songs this chord is seldom to be found. But in more sophisticated, colourful chord sequences it appears as a kind of spice. You find him appearing almost always before the G^7 or G^9 as his harbinger, his herald.

As the combination Dm^7 - G^7 (or G^9) is the most commonly used module in standards, I would like to show you all the different ways in which it is used and

reveal to you how to incorporate it in order to create the most interesting sounds. To do this, we need to take a closer look at G^7 and G^9.

When we play standards, blues, gospel, jazz and so on, we avoid playing G^7 as far as possible, as it produces a rather straight, plain, primitive sound. For such types of piano music we prefer to use the extended form, G^9. It is the same chord as G^7 only with a third added on top, like a little hat.

In folk melodies or Christmas carols on the other hand, we would use the simple G^7. It consists of the first, third and fifth steps of the G major scale, i.e. *g*, *b* and *d*. In addition, comes the foreign note, indicated in the symbol: the *f* borrowed from the scale of C major.

In the bass we of course play *g*. Here are its four positions:

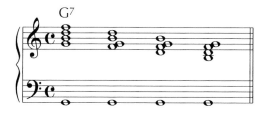

Let's take a look at the last eight bars of the Christmas carol 'Silent Night'. Here we find G^7 in all its inversions.

Now we shall experiment a little and listen to the immediate difference produced if we add the herald Dm^7 within the last four bars of this song before the G^7. The sound is much more interesting.

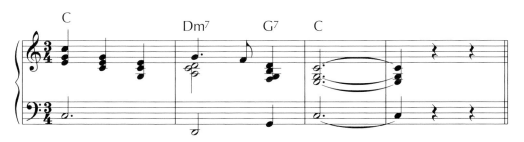

Please turn back to page 52, where you will find the module C - C° followed by Dm^7 - G^9. The last bar of this example, with the Dm^7 - G^9, is very similar to the Dm^7 - G^7 in 'Silent Night', except that G^9 is used rather than G^7. And what is the difference between G^7 and G^9? It is just that one note is added, the **a**! If you add an **a** somewhere – anywhere – to a G^7 chord, you get a G^9. The **a** is the (2nd and) 9th step of the G major scale. So, you can see that it is not difficult to produce a more interesting sound.

In our examples from standards and pop hits, we will soon usually replace G^7 with G^9, that means we will add an **a** some-where. As well as this, whenever possible, the left hand plays an interval of a seventh in the bass, that is the **g** and the seventh – **f**. This creates the best sound. In the G^9 alternative given in brackets, we have left out the note **d** to show that an interesting sound can still be produced when a note is left out.

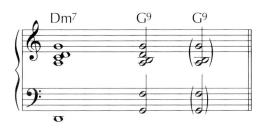

This combination of chords, Dm^7 - G^9, should be mastered in all inversions. To do this we shall take practical examples from passages that occur like this, or in a similar way, in standards. Let's look at a commonly used version of the chord-module C - C° - Dm^7 - G^9:

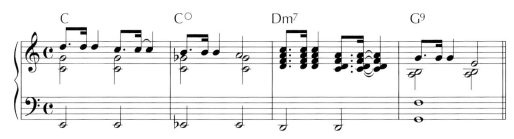

That sounds really nice, doesn't it? I hope that you won't be confused if the components *g*, *b*, *d*, *f* and *a* of G^9 appear in a different order. You will notice that in the G^9 of the last bar the note *d* is missing. We are now concentrating on the sound and often it is just as good or perhaps even better if a note is omitted. Now let's look at another melody that sounds good with the module Dm^7 - G^9:

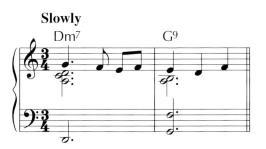

It is an old melody, which you may remember. Now we will try a passage in which the G^9 appears in the melody:

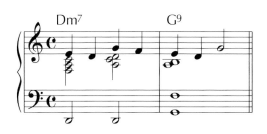

That was an example in which the melody was at a lower pitch: from *d* to treble-clef *g*. Here is another example where the melody appears in this pitch-range:

The difference between the two chords Dm^7 and G^9 in the right hand is very slight. Only the *c* of the first chord goes down to *b* in the second, so the difference is a

58

semitone. All the other right-hand notes stay the same.

The Dm^7 can be added beneath a melodic note at almost any pitch. There is a problem only with **b**, which we shall discuss shortly. The G^9 is also difficult to bring in when the melodic note is **b**. If we use it, we have to play the lower two right-hand notes with the thumb. When the melody is at this pitch, it is more practical to use the straightforward G^7. With the following melodic construction you can hardly hear the difference.

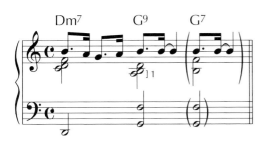

Here is another example where the pitch of the melody is around **b**. It is a melody that you probably know. Here, too, it is better if we use the simple G^7 so that it is not so difficult to play. Besides, there is an **a** in the melody with the G^7 chord in the first bar so the G^9 character makes an appearance.

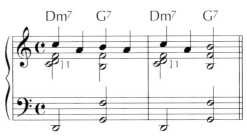

When the melody appears in the note-range **a** to **c**, the G^9 may easily be used. The **a** fits in well and is easy to play. Even if the melody rises up to **e** you can simply play the Dm^7 - G^9 module like this:

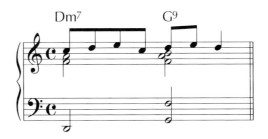

Again, this was a case where the symbol could have been Dm rather than Dm^7 as the ^{7} (**c**) is played in the melody and therefore need not necessarily be mentioned in the symbol.

Perhaps it would be a good idea and would help give an overview if we review the Dm^7 - G^9 module at each pitch:

The chords are probably not yet familiar to you and will not feel comfortable to play. But you don't have to start and practise them right away, as we shall be replacing some of them with others that will be easier to play if the melody goes to a position where we might have problems with Dm^7 or G^9. You can see, for example, in the fifth bar of the musical example above, that when the melodic note is *b*, you cannot play the complete Dm^7 chord as this would sound dissonant. The rather strange-sounding *c* is played only briefly so that it does not destroy the sound. For G^9 in the same bar, as previously mentioned, you have to play the two lower notes at the same time with the thumb of the right hand. This table shows you the basic construction of the two chords in different positions and how to play them.

We shall now proceed in a rather unusual way, from the complicated to the straightforward, with the aim of producing the richest and most colourful sound in the simplest possible way. To do this we will look once again at the secondary form of G^7 or G^9: $G^{7/6}$. If there is a *g* in the melody, it is particularly easy and effective to play:

This can also be called G^{13}, as the *e* is the 6th and 13th step of the G major scale.

If a Dm^7 is required before the $G^{7/6}$ (at the same pitch) then this is the best form to use:

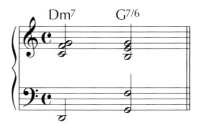

You can see here that in the bass of a G^7 or G^9 form we usually find the interval of a seventh, **g** - **f**. So if the melodic note is **g** and you want to harmonize it with Dm^7 - G^7 or G^9, you would usually play Dm^7 - $G^{7/6}$ as in the previous example. These chords are easier to play and you might like to practise them a few times. But do not worry, we will find them again and again in melodies from now on.

To achieve the aim of playing from memory, from now on try to get used to relying on your ear. Of course I will have to continue to give you the musical examples in written form and you will need to read them; this is unfortunately unavoidable for the time being. But please always listen carefully to the sound of each chord you play. This is particularly important. This is the only way you will eventually free yourself from the printed music.

If you listen to the sound of the Dm^7 in the previous example, it probably gives the impression of a certain dissonance; a dissonance that requires resolution. You will notice a transitory quality: you cannot rest on this Dm^7 for long, it is not an ending chord, but rather it presses on towards a G^7 chord. It is for this reason that we might compare it with a herald.

Now listen to the sound of $G^{7/6}$. And then exchange this chord for the G^9 with **g** in the melody. You will find this in the chord table on page 60. Listen to this G^9 chord very carefully too. These jazzy chords might all sound a bit strange to you. But you will get used to them in time and you will find them more colourful then the rather ordinary chords that you have been playing until now.

You now have enough experience with chords to continue the melodic example given on page 58.

Penthouse Serenade (Will Jason/Val Burton)
© 1931 by Famous Music Corp., 1619 Broadway, New York, N. Y.

There are a few things to be said about this. From this example you might come to the wrong conclusion, that the C chord is always played with an *e* in the bass instead of a *c*. This is an exceptional case because it is followed immediately by C° and we want to make use of the bass moving from *e* to *e flat*. In the second system of the previous example we find two bars in succession with almost the same melody. The two bars would be almost identical if we added a G^9 after the Dm^7 in the first and second bars. Or $G^{7/6}$ in both cases. But here we use G^9 in the first bar and $G^{7/6}$ in the second to bring in some variety.

G major scale: *g, b, d*. We dress this simplest of the G chords up a bit by pushing up the fifth step by a semitone. So we turn the *d* into *d sharp*. If we play a *g* in the bass, as we should, we have the chord that is indicated by G^+. But if you add the seventh-interval *g - f*, it sounds even better. It is then called $G^{7/+}$ or $G^{7/+5}$, $G^{7/5+}$ or $G^{7/5aug}$.

You will certainly remember the C^+ in the C family. The $^+$ means simply that the fifth step of the C major scale is raised by a semitone. Similarly, in G^+ the fifth step of the G major scale is raised by a semitone. So we take the basic G major chord, i.e. the first, third and fifth steps of the

This chord has a very distinctive sound. Let your ear get used to it so that you will recognize the sound in a melody as soon as it appears.

Now we will look at a few melodic sequences in which this chord appears. We already have a few modules at hand with which we can work.

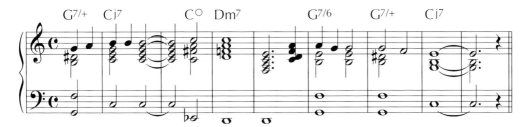

Congratulations! You already know enough complicated chords to understand a song that sounds complicated. You are now able to decipher the symbols of difficult chord systems such as $G^{7/6}$, $G^{7/+}$, Dm^7, Cj^7, etc. As time goes on your use of these chords and chord sequences will become fluent. You need only be patient; and I must take care not to move on too quickly and to support everything I introduce with plenty of examples.

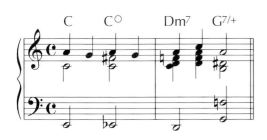

The above example shows once again the modules C - C° and Dm^7 - $G^{7/+}$. Instead of using $G^{7/+}$ for the last chord, you could use one of the other G^7 variants such as, for example, G^9 or $G^{7/6}$.

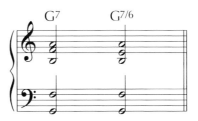

For the G^9 with the note **a** in the melody, we write G^7 as the melodic note need not be added to the symbol. But of course this chord has the G^9 sound as the **a** is played in the melody and completes the chord. Do not forget to listen carefully when you exchange the last chord ($G^{7/+}$) of the last example but one for the two chords shown in the last example. Notice the subtle difference in sound and try to remember it.

As I have mentioned several times, the construction of chords depends on the melody. If, for example, in a Dm^7 chord the melody note is **c**, we can play Dm^7 in its purest form: **d** - **f** - **a** - **c**.

Even if the melody note is **f**, **a** or **d** we still have the pure Dm⁷ sound, only the order of the notes is changed around. In this case we talk about inversions of the chord.

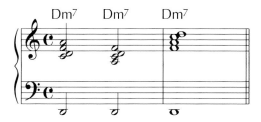

We need only take care when an **e**, **g** or **b** turns up in the melody, as these notes are not components of Dm⁷ and so bring a strange sound into play. I have just mentioned the difficulty of having a **b** in the melody with Dm⁷ (and also with G⁹). If you play all the notes at once it does not sound very good.

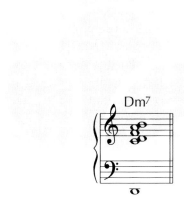

There are too many dissonances here. There are only two possibilities in this case. Either you can leave the seventh (**c**) out and play a simple D minor chord, which becomes Dm⁶ with the **b** in the melody. Or you can play the seventh afterwards and pass on immediately to the next chord.

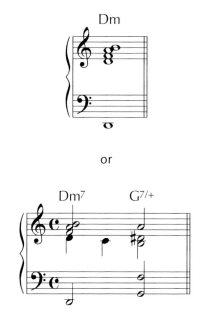

or

The foreign melody notes **g** and **e**, however, go very well with Dm⁷. They do not produce a dissonance, but rather an exotic sound.

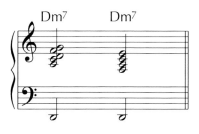

The same thing applies in the construction of most other chords. If the melody happens to be one of the notes of the chord, there is no problem. But if one of the other two or three notes that do not belong to the chord appear in the melody, you must know how to deal with this by using the simpler basic chord; or by playing the most dissonant note only very briefly.

Of these rather more complicated chord-types that we have encountered on the last few pages as a kind of extension of the normal G^7, not all appear in every position. $G^{7/6}$, for example, is only used instead of G^9 if there is a **g**, or perhaps an **a**, in the melody.

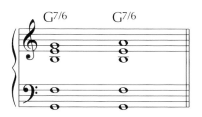

It is similar with $G^{7/+}$. This chord is used even when there is a **g** in the melody and perhaps also when the melody note is **d sharp**, **a** or **b**. Otherwise it is not used.

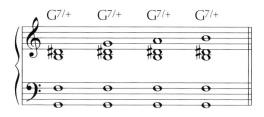

Here is another example of a melodic sequence which makes full use of $G^{7/+}$. Please don't forget to listen to the distinctive sound of the raised fifth step ($^+$) of the scale.

Our chords now sound very professional as professionals use just these chords and no others. We just have to get used to them and use them whenever possible. Let us now see what happens when a melody rises by step instead of descending.

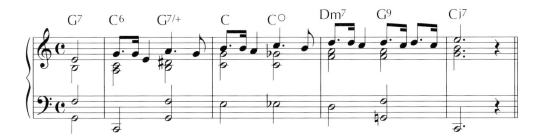

Let us take a closer look at the chord symbols of this example. First of all there is a G^7. It is not necessary to write $G^{7/6}$ here as the sixth step of the G major scale (*e*) appears in the melody. The components of G^7 (*g, b, d, f*) are not all present as the *d* is missing. The space between the notes *b* and *e* in the right hand is too small to fit in the *d*, so we have left it out. In the next chord we have added the 6th to the C chord. You have already encountered the $G^{7/+}$ in this position. Then comes the C - C° module, with which you are also familiar. Finally we have the ending module Dm^7 - G^9 - Cj^7. The module Dm^7 - G^7 - C has been slightly altered. In the place of G^7 we find G^9, which also belongs to the G^7 group, as does $G^{7/6}$ or $G^{7/+}$. You can see this from the seventh intervals in the bass of these chords. I hope that you do not mind having the Cj^7 at the end instead of a simple C chord.

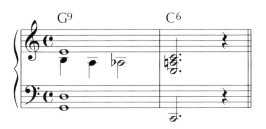

fore becomes *a flat*. This chord does not present any particular difficulties as it is usually used only in one position, that is when there is an *e* in the melody or occasionally when there is a *d, f* or *g*.

G^{9-} is a melancholy chord that creates a little sadness and is therefore not really suited to quick passages. You should use it in a slow, measured way. It sounds best if you play it as a transition from *b* down to *a flat*.

There is another outsider that belongs to the G^7 group. We play the interval of a seventh in the bass, *g - f*, with this chord too. It is called G^{9-}, which tells us that it is actually G^9 (*g, b, d, f, a*), with the ninth step lowered by a semitone. The *a* there-

It is not difficult to memorize these passages. You couldn't really play this transition any other way unless, of course, you play all the notes together, as at the beginning of the following song.

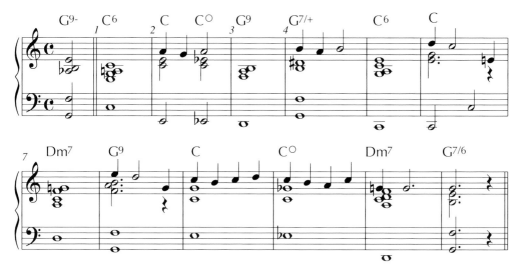

A Fine Romance (Jerome Kern/Dorothy Fields)
© 1936 by T. B. Harms Company, New York
Chappell & Co., Ltd., 50, New Bond Street, London W1 & Sydney

That is an attractive melody with very interesting chords. Of course, in spite of this, the whole thing still sounds rather boring because we have just added the chords beneath the melody. There is no drive and no rhythm in this arrangement and so the effect is not very expressive. Apart from this the piece consists only of C chords and only two modules: Dm^7 - G^7 and C - C°. It is clear that this must be rather unsatisfactory.

We must, however, proceed in small steps. I know that we all want to see great results immediately, when we embark on something new. But you must have patience. We cannot create our wonderful culinary concoction until the end of our journey. At the moment we are still gathering our ingredients.

You must not forget, that people who make a living from this kind of playing have often spent decades working on their style until they found out what you find presented here on a plate. So please have some patience.

Now, back to our previous musical example. Learn the first two bars off by heart as these are frequently encountered.

If you look at the bass of the C chords you will see that in the bass we sometimes find a *c*, sometimes an *e*. So when should we play a *c* and when should we play an *e*? If an ordinary C chord appears (C, C^6, Cj^7) in a bar on its own and is not followed by C°, we play a *c* in the bass. It is only when the module C - C° appears that we take the third in the bass, that is, the *e*, so that we can descend to the *e flat* in the bass for the following C°, which always sounds good.

It would perhaps be a good idea to learn the last two bars of the musical example as well. You will come across this Dm^7 - $G^{7/6}$ combination in many passages. Of course this song does not end here, but it goes on to use chords that we have not yet encountered. We will present the rest of the piece when we have mastered the missing elements.

I can well imagine that you can't wait to be presented, at last, with a complete song instead of being given little bits and pieces. Please have just a little more patience. It will not be long before we present the first complete song. Before this, we will look at a standard that you might well know. It is an old hit from the twenties that is often spiced up, and seems as though it will be around for ever: 'Just a Gigolo'. Here, too, we encounter the modules C - C° and Dm^7 - G^7 once again.

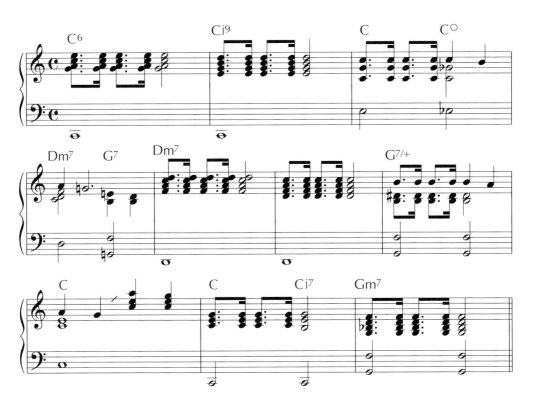

Schöner Gigolo, armer Gigolo (Leonello Casucci/Julius Brammer)
© 1929 by Wiener Bohème Verlag GmbH, Berlin – München

Stop! We have to stop in the middle of this piece! You have not yet encountered this Gm^7 chord that has suddenly appeared.

Gm⁷

At the beginning, you heard that the third step of the minor scale is lowered by a semitone.

If we now want to use Gm⁶ or Gm⁷ we have to add the 6th or 7th step to the basic triad of Gm.

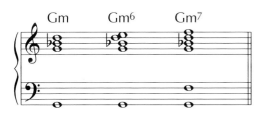

With the knowledge you have already acquired about chords there will certainly no longer be anything mysterious about these constructions. The only thing that might appear a bit strange is the seventh in the bass of the Gm⁷ chord. Until now we used this interval only with G⁷ and its variants G⁹, G⁷/⁶ and G⁷/⁺. Depending on the arrangement of the chord, it can sound very nice with many minor seventh chords. We now already have a few good chords that we can use with a single-note melody, to make it worth listening to. As an example, let us take the note *g* – which is the most frequently occuring melody note in songs in C major.

It would be a good idea to memorize this passage so that you can use it later for improvising.

Gm⁷, like Dm⁷, sounds good in all of its four different positions.

We have seen that we may consider Dm⁷ a member of the group of C chords as its components appear in the C major scale (*d, f, a, c*) and it usually appears with members of the C family. It is similar with Gm⁷. With its components *g, b flat, d, f* it is related to the F major scale. It belongs to the F family and is most at home in this key.

The same things apply with regard to the arrangement of the chord beneath the melodic notes. Gm^7 is only presented with a problem if the melody note falls rather unfortunately on the seventh step of the F major scale, that is on the *e*. We can only improve matters by playing either a simple Gm (without the seventh) or by only briefly playing the seventh.

or

Apart from this it goes very well with every note of F major.

Here we have used the seventh-interval only when the melody note is *g*. But this is not a strict rule. You could play either a *g* or *g* and *f* in the bass with any of the melody notes. It is partly a question of personal taste in selecting the sounds you prefer. I would like to stress that it is important for you to rely less and less on the written notes, to listen to the sounds and to experiment.

Perhaps you have been wondering why I have dwelt for so long on the procedures and roots of chord formation. This is because we are dealing with rules that apply to all the chords of all the other scales.

So, for example, it does not matter whether we are dealing with a Dm^7 chord, Am^7, Fm^7 or any other minor seventh chord, they all have the same characteristic in that they function as a herald for the seventh chord that lies four steps higher.

So Dm^7 - G^7 (or their variants) form a fixed module. Similarly, Gm^7 - C^7 (or their variants) form a fixed module. Let us have a look at this:

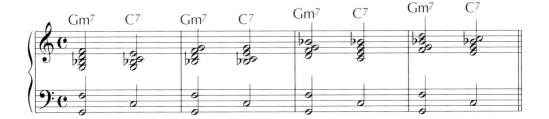

We have been flexible again here and this time we have used the interval of a seventh in the bass with all the Gm^7 chords, but with C^7 we have left it out. You know that we are allowed to arrange chords as we wish as long as we use the notes indicated in the symbol, either in full or in part, and do not use any that are not indicated. It does not matter which order we play them in or how they are positioned.

We are just about to acquire another chord to use with a **g** in the melody – C^9 – which we can add to our sequence of related chords.

Gm^7 here functions as the herald for C^9. I explained in Chapter 1 that C^9 is a C^7 with another third added on top, i.e. the **d** – the ninth step of the C major scale. So you create C^9 when you add a **d** to a C^7 chord, in an appropriate place.

C^7 and its variants (C^9, $C^{7/6}$, $C^{7/+}$) belong to the F family from which they have borrowed the foreign component **b flat**. They are all drawn towards the F chord. It does not matter whether it is F, F^6, F^{j7} or F^{j9}; they are all pure chords that use only the components of the F major scale. On top of this, C^7 also leads to the F minor chords Fm, Fm^6 and Fm^7.

It would be best to take a look now at all these F chords in the different positions in which they appear. First of all there is the normal F major chord: the first, third and fifth steps of the F major scale.

With F, F^6, F^{j7} or F^{j9} of course there is an *f* in the bass – not a seventh interval! F^6 takes in the 6th step of the F major scale as well: *d*. If you take a closer look at F^6, you will be surprised to see that it is identical to Dm^7 in the right hand. You can only distinguish them from their bass notes.

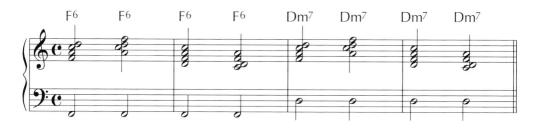

F^{j7} is not quite as adaptable as other chords. This applies of course to all ^{j7} chords. It can only really be used in three positions at the most.

As you cannot play this with one hand, we have to divide the F^{j9} between the bass and the right hand.

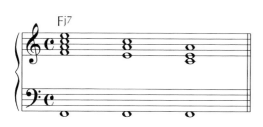

In the last two chords you can only tell from the bass that we are dealing with F^{j7}. If there was an *a* in the bass, the chord would be called Am (A minor). We have not talked about this yet, but we will soon come to it.

F^{j9} – like all other ^{j9} chords – can only be used in one position. You would change the sound if you tried to force it into another position.

The ^{j9} chords appear quite rarely. In spite of this we need to know about them and be able to recognize them. The most commonly used F chords are F^6 and F^{j7}.

There remain three Fm chords (F minor chords) that take their components from the F minor scale: Fm, Fm^6 and Fm^7.

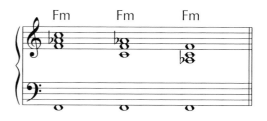

Fm⁶ is an interesting chord that can be put to good use at certain parts of a melody. It is also flexible and can be used with any melody note. Here its four inversions:

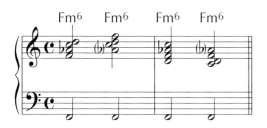

And, to finish, here is Fm⁷ in its four inversions. Like all the m⁷ chords, it also serves as herald for some other chord – which we will deal with later.

That is enough theory. Now we must try to fit these chords to melodies and link some of them to produce new modules. Perhaps we should begin by extending our chord sequence on the melody note *g* with Fʲ⁷ and Fm⁶. We now have a series of seven chords in succession that harmonize the note *g*. All of them sound exquisite and interesting.

Series such as this will be extremely useful for our improvisations later on. They also serve another purpose. It often happens that a note (for example *g*) is held on for a long time – often for two bars or more – at the end of a musical phrase (instrumental or sung). It would be rather monotonous if we had only one chord to play for this sustained melody note. But using a sequence, such as the one we have just seen, we can present a harmonic transition to please any ear.

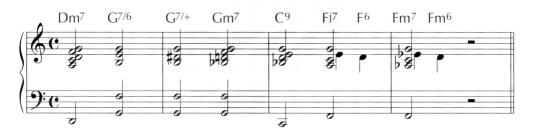

Our palette of colours is gradually becoming richer as we now have two new modules at our disposal: Gm^7 - C^7 (or its variants C^9, $C^{7/6}$ and $C^{7/+}$), as well as the module F - Fm^7 - Fm^6. I'll just introduce briefly the variants C^9, $C^{7/6}$ and $C^{7/+}$ in their most commonly used inversions.

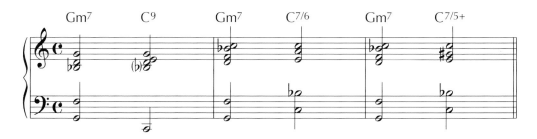

These chords are of course now new and unfamiliar to you. We will gradually incorporate them in our melodies and as time goes on you will get used to using them. In the right hand, the differences between these chords (Cm^7 and C^9 or $C^{7/6}$ or $C^{7/+}$) are slight, which is rather confusing. In the beginning it will be necessary to work out whether it is really Cm^7, C^9, $C^{7/6}$ or $C^{7/+}$. To do this you will usually have to ignore the melody note, which is often a note foreign to the basic chord. I realize, of course, that chord progressions such as the one just introduced are not easy to pick up immediately and will take you a little while to get used to playing. It is only when an individual module occurs in a particular inversion frequently in a song that you will get used to it so that you have it at your finger-tips to add at a certain point of the melody. Let us now take a look at a melody in which the module Gm^7 - C^7 occurs at the beginning and the module F - Fm at the end.

You will have noticed that we are beginning to link individual modules together. In the previous example the module F - Fm follows the module Gm⁷ - C⁷/⁵⁺. In the same way you can of course link the modules F - Fm and C - C° and Dm⁷ - G.

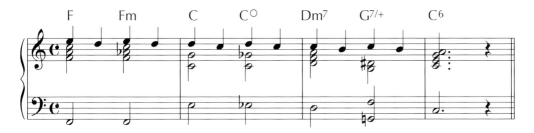

In this way you can produce a whole series which you can in time memorize and which you will then be able to use for playing freely, for improvising or to fill in gaps. If we encounter a certain module in a chord progression, we will then often know in advance what is coming next.

Perhaps you can still remember the Fj⁷ chord, about which we said on page 72 that in the right hand it resembles the Am chord and that you can only identify it from the *f* in the bass. If there was an *a* in the bass it would be Am.

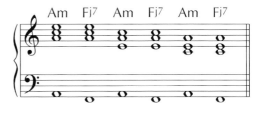

Am (A minor) consists of the first, third and fifth steps of the A minor scale, i.e. *a*, *c*, *e*. You can also regard this as a member of the C family as each of the three notes appear in the C major scale. We can make good use of this new sound in the company of the chords we already know. Listen to its distinctive sound.

This chord progression and transition in the bass appear like this or in a similar form in many melodies, for example, in the French song 'La Mer' by Charles Trenet.

Am^6 and Am^7 are unproblematic chords and may easily be inverted or rearranged.

Am^7 is again a chord that has identical notes in the right hand to another chord: C^6. If you play a *c* in the bass you have C^6. However, if there is an *a* in the bass the chord symbol would be Am^7.

It is interesting to find out the chord for which Am^7 serves as a herald. As we have already heard, minor seventh chords are great announcers that prepare the way for an important chord that follows on immediately (some form of seventh chord). You just have to go up four steps or down five steps, then you will find the great master that has been announced by the herald. In this case, D^7, which uses the first, third and fifth steps of the D major scale and the false seventh, *c*.

Usually, however, we use one of the variants – D^9, $D^{7/6}$ or $D^{7/+}$, which sound rather more interesting.

With these chords we now have another module: Am^7 - D^7 (or one of its variants – D^9, D$^{7/6}$ or D$^{7/+}$). This module enriches our choice of sounds immensely. We will soon encounter this in many examples and will soon become familiar with it.

You have now been presented with a great chunk of theory about chords, which is impossible to absorb all at once. It will take time to remember everything in your mind and in your fingers. We are now equipped, however, to harmonize complete songs from now on. There are just a few things missing before we can play everything we would like to play. These few elements will be added gradually, one after another, to the knowledge you have already acquired, whenever a suitable moment arises.

For the time being we just have to take in one more chord, the diminished. It consists of a series of minor thirds and there are only three kinds altogether.

The fourth, which we have added here, is just the same as the first, only in a different position. So there are actually

only three. You already know C°. D♭° and D° are the other two. As you can use any note of the chord in the bass, these three chords can appear in a symbol with any note name.

So in place of C°, the same chord might be found with the symbol E♭°, F♯°, or A°. But that need not bother us. You could say that these diminished chords with their distinctive, interesting sound, are very easy to deal with.

So, we can now play our first song from beginning to end. It is a well-known, slow composition by Duke Ellington and is called 'Solitude'. On page 63 you were given eight bars of the beginning of this beautiful song, with slight variations. Now I will show you the complete song with the original chords by Duke Ellington, who one could not say wrote simple songs. On the contrary, in the jazz world his compositions are regarded as the most colourful and complicated written in his time.

This standard is very slow and sustained. You can therefore take your time. Please remember, too, that this is a sad song.

77

Solitude (Duke Ellington/Eddie de Lange/Irving Mills)
© 1934 by American Academy of Musik, Inc.
Copyright renewed 1962 by American Academy of Musik, Inc.
and Scarsdale Music Corp.

78

The first eight bars are almost identical to the second eight bars. In the third bar, however, Duke Ellington puts in a Dm^7 chord, whereas in bar 11 he used D^7 with the same melody. We have already encountered most of the chord combinations in 'Solitude' in one way or another. The exceptions are $G^{7/4}$ at the beginning of bar 13 and $C\sharp^\circ$ in bar 23. $G^{7/4}$ is a G^7, with the fourth step of the G major scale added instead of the third, i.e. *c*. $C\sharp^\circ$ is no mystery either. It is the diminished chord on *c sharp*. Above the *c sharp*, layers of minor thirds are added: *c sharp, e, g, b flat*. Here, Duke Ellington has used this chord with the melody note *a*. We must therefore leave out the *g* so that the notes of the chord are not too close together, which would create a rather clumsy effect.

Now, that is really enough theoretical observation of one chord or another. We are now going to enter a phase of practice, in which we will recreate everything that we have encountered so far with different melodic examples. This is the only way to get used to playing one module after another before we get to know any more.

Now I have a rather unusual request to make: please learn to play 'Solitude' from memory! I know that such a request is bound to be rather unpopular. You didn't buy such a method of learning to play music by ear to be told to learn to play a piece from this book off by heart.

But you should not learn the piece in the usual way, i.e. by playing the piece from the printed music five times in succession. No, take it apart and look at this piece in terms of its chord construction. In this way you will look at the up-beat and first bar as a standard module $G^{7/5+}$ - C^{j7} and take note of the sound of this module as well as the position and fingering of the notes in each hand. This is much more fun than simply reading notes. Then go on to the next combination, Am^7 - Dm^7, and so on.

Good, it will take you some time to work at 'Solitude' until you can play it all the way through from memory. It is worth the trouble though because you have now prepared all the individual chord constructions and you will have plenty of opportunities to use them again and again on other occasions. You are not trying to learn like a parrot, who is able to say something off by heart without having any idea of its meaning. No, you are trying to learn something, the construction of which you understand.

All the chord constructions and modules that appear in 'Solitude' will be discussed and used again in the context of other melodic examples until they become second nature to us.

To end this chapter, perhaps I should briefly draw your attention to a feature that we have not yet mentioned, and which we will deal with later. We come across this for the first time in bar 20 of 'Solitude'.

As in this bar, you will often find that in the accompaniment of songs (here in the bass), single notes appear without being indicated in the figuration system. The slight sound variations that they produce are not given in the chord symbols above the melody. These are actually only ornaments. Ornaments can be added, but are not essential. The chord symbols, however, show only the essentials.

CHAPTER 4

AWAY FROM THE EYE AND OVER TO THE EAR

If you watch people in the street for a long time, you might notice old people walking with a stick although they do not really need it. The doctor may have told them that their leg is better, yet they continue to use the walking stick. You can tell that they do not need it as they are not leaning on it; simply swinging it around a bit.

Why do they do that? It is simply the force of habit. They have got used to a crutch and believe that they cannot manage without it. You can understand this.

It is just as easy to understand that people who have been playing the piano from printed music for years might think that they have no talent for free improvisation and can only play by reading the notes. Their brain cells and nerve cords have been trained for a long time to take the easier way of decoding certain symbols from a piece of paper with the eyes, and

transforming this pattern into nerve impulses which cause the ten fingers to move in a particular way.

Now we must gradually get used to a second way of playing. This way is a kind of endless loop. We press the keys with our fingers in a particular position and at the same time listen intently to the sound that our fingers have produced. Now the sound that our ear hears requires another sound – perhaps it was the first chord of a module that needs the second chord. And now the impulse comes from the ear, bringing our fingers into another position to produce this new sound. And so it goes on, from the ear to the fingers and from the fingers to the ear.

Of course this process is only consciously experienced to begin with. In time the subconscious takes over so that the interaction ear–hand-position–ear takes place automatically. But it takes a while to get to this stage.

Let us now take the example of a typical sound that we no longer want to approach by reading, but rather experience by ear:

the + (the fifth step is raised by a semi-tone). Let us take G+ or G7/+.

Here we have the chord in almost all the positions it appears. Play the passage a dozen times in the most comfortable position, as indicated by the fingering given. The ear and hand should feel good while you let the sound of the G7/+ be absorbed by your ear and grasp its specific character. You must become so familiar with this sound that you will hear it immediately in pieces of music that you listen to on cassette, CD, radio or whatever.

In future you would not need a melody to be presented in a fully notated form as before. As you now know exactly how to play and what the chord will sound like when G7/+ appears, the following written form would suffice:

or it might appear in this form:

or like this:

84

You can of course also break up this chord.
The sound remains the same.

Another of the many possibilities is this:

How often, and when, you play the seventh interval in the bass on **g** is entirely up to you. You should perhaps – for example, when quavers appear in the melody – use it rather sparingly.

If we add C^6 somewhere in the previous example, instead of G$^{7/+}$, we would have a module. It is the combination G$^{7/+}$ - C^6 that appears, in some form, in many, many songs. Experience this purely by ear.

We could also place the C^6 chord at the end:

Please make sure that you include C^6 in the ear–hand-position–ear process. To do this it is necessary to find a comfortable fingering for C^6. The fingers should almost automatically fall to C^6 from $G^{7/+}$. This needs a bit of practice. By the way, if you look closely at the melody in the two previous musical examples, you will see that we could just as well have written C instead of C^6. The sixth step appears in the melody and did not really need to be mentioned in the chord symbol. You will recall the indication 'n.c.' mentioned at the beginning, meaning 'no chord'.

Now let us look at another fully-notated example of the change from C^6 - $G^{7/+}$, in which a C^{j7} also appears. This time, experiment a bit with the bass notes. Listen to the sound you achieve when you play the bass notes with each melodic note. Or what it sounds like when you play the bass note or notes just once in a bar.

Now change the rhythm of the melody as you wish. Perhaps like this:

Or play the whole thing in 3/4 time. It doesn't matter how you play C^6 - $G^{7/+}$ - C^{j7}, at the moment we are only interested in the ear–hand-position–ear relationship.

You must listen to the sound in the way that a connoisseur of wine savours a particularly delicious wine.

Slowly

And now let us look again at one of the musical examples from page 84 in a slightly different form. We do not need to add the bass notes as we already know which notes to play.

Let us now concentrate on the sound produced by the $^j9$ chord. The C^{j9} is surrounded by C major chords: C^6, C and C^{j7}. With the low *c* in the bass the sound of these four C chord types is very similar and closely related.

Here is another similar example:

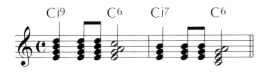

Please listen carefully to this sound. And then listen to the same melody when we add another interesting sound: the C - C° module that we encountered earlier. Perhaps you remember that with this module we make an exception in the bass and, instead of playing *c* with the C chord, we play *e* – which is of course also part of this chord. Finally, we go down to *e flat* in the bass.

We are now going to work through several examples using the C - C° module so that our ear will grow accustomed to it and we will then be able to add it whenever it fits with the melody. Everything we do now is a revision of our visual knowledge of the different chords and chord modules, with the aim of developing a feeling for the ear–hand-position–ear process.

In this example we have added the extending modules Dm^7 - G$^{7/6}$ and G$^{7/+}$ - C^{j7}, which almost always occur in this order. Here is another similar line:

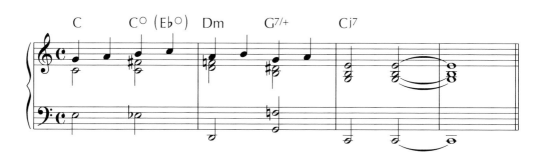

You will realize that we are not dealing with inflexible progressions. Depending on the flow of the melody, our modules apear with slight variations. In the previous example, instead of the Dm^7 - G$^{7/6}$ module, we used a simple Dm that led immediately to G$^{7/+}$. In the bass I gave the D minor chord a low **d**. Why not? You could of course add the **d** at the top. You are now no longer just reading the notes but you are creating sound. This experimentation with sound requires you to try out slight variations. It might be that you change the melody slightly; or that you play the bass lower or higher, or that you leave out or add a certain module.

Let us take the melody of the example before last and change it slightly by adding a semitone between the whole-tone steps or by introducing a little ornamentation here and there.

Or we could apply the same principle in the last bar as in the first:

Please experiment in this way with all melodic examples from now on. Decorate the melody a little or change it slightly. Now you are beginning to improvise!

Here is another way of varying the melody:

Please don't forget to listen intently to all these sounds – to the bass, the modules, the little changes to the melody.

Now experiment a little with the bass. Decide whether you prefer the bass transition from **e - e flat** in the module C - C° at the pitch shown until now, or whether you prefer it played an octave lower. I would advise you not to play the seventh interval at too low a pitch. Only single bass notes sound good when they are very low. In the previous musical example you will have seen that after the C° symbol I added another possible figuration in brackets, i.e. E♭°. You know that the diminished chord C° consists of **c - e flat - g flat - a** and that any of these notes could be used in the bass as the diminished E♭° or diminished G♭° or A°

are the same chord and consist of the same elements. You can therefore give this chord four different symbols. It would be best always to give the symbol of the note that appears in the bass. In this case we give the symbol E♭°. Then you know at least which note to play in the bass.

The third of the previously mentioned possibilities of experimenting with a melody involves exchanging or adding modules. In the previous chord progression you could, for example, play $G^{7/+}$ after the Dm^7 and in the next bar add $G^{7/6}$ after the C^{j7}.

Apart from this, you could always play the whole thing with different rhythms. You needn't play according to any scheme or give it a great deal of thought but simply try things out.

We now want to look at a new module. In the musical examples on the last pages we always had the final C^{j7} chord with the melodic note **e** and a low **c** in the bass. Please play this now a few times and listen to its distinctive sound.

We could just as effectively use C^6 in the right hand.

It is not the same sound but it is a similarly final-sounding chord. That is, a sound that does not necessarily need another to follow. In spite of this, we want to continue on towards A^7 or A^9 because it sounds so good. As A^7 and A^9 are so-called seventh chords, we send a herald ahead.

We have already heard that the minor seventh chord that lies four steps below the chord we are aiming for is an excellent herald. To lead towards A^7 or A^9 we can therefore put in Em^7 (**e** is four notes below **a**). But there is another herald that also guarantees a nice transition, that is the minor sixth or seventh or ordinary minor chord that lies just one note below the chord for which we are aiming. I have intentionally chosen the order minor sixth, minor seventh, normal minor chord as the minor sixth creates the best transition, the minor seventh quite a pleasant one and the normal minor produces a quite acceptable transition. So to reach our target A^7 (A^9, $A^{7/6}$, $A^{7/+}$, A^{9-}, etc.) we could insert the m^6 that lies one note lower, that is Gm^6 (see page 69). Just listen to how good this module sounds:

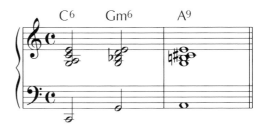

As the A chords have not yet appeared in our book, perhaps we should first take a look at them in all their different forms and inversions. The A major chords use notes of the A major scale as their components.

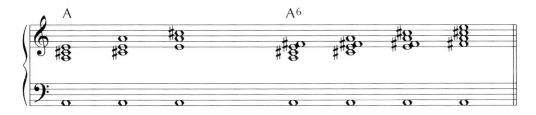

All the seventh chords on *a*, i.e. all the A chords for which we use the interval of a seventh in the bass, use the seventh step that has been taken from a foreign scale.

The *g* does not appear in A major. It comes from the scale of D major and so the seventh chords on *a* lead towards the D chords.

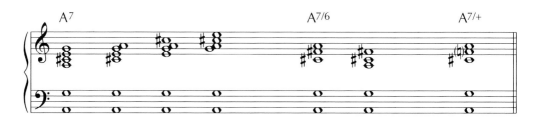

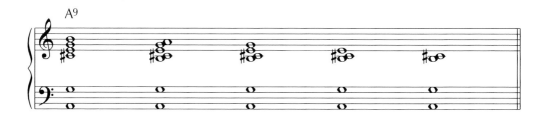

Play these chords a few times now so that your ear gets used to the sound and your fingers get used to the hand positions. Of course we will take care not to use all of them immediately. We will select just one or two of them. We will gradually add the others into our chord sequences here and there. We can look them up in the table above.

Let us now take a look at our newly-created module C⁶ - Gm⁶ - A⁹ and, above all, listen very carefully to this succession

of sounds. In addition to this, we must try to find the most effective positions to make the chords easy to play.

If we now apply this module to a melody, for example the one on page 88 that begins with *d - c*, it immediately produces a wonderful harmonic progression.

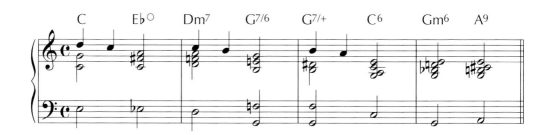

I would now like to ask you to practise this little melody a bit, until your fingers can play it easily and until you can play it completely by ear. You should concentrate more and more on playing little harmonic progressions, consisting of modules linked together, in a certain rational way, letting the ear absorb the specific sounds. And you must do this for as long and as intensively as necessary until these progressions have settled down into your sub-conscious and can be recalled at any time.

If you master several such progressions, you will gather a supply of modules, or even chains of modules, that always appear in one song or another. You will soon become familiar with these extremely useful components of songs and so you will be able to hear when to use them without any difficulty and your fingers will easily find the right notes.

As soon as you can play these few bars easily and without the printed music, we will finish the whole thing off with a nice ending. For this we will take an A^9 chord, add a few Dm^7 inversions and end with a nice G^9 - G^{9-} - C^6 module that appears at the end of thousands of songs.

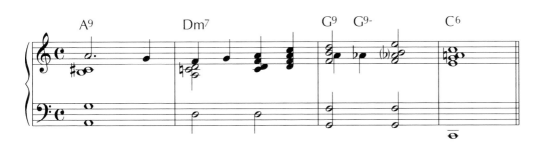

Now work through the whole little section of the song until you have forgotten all the notes that were written down and you can let your fingers play freely.

In time we must of course try to extend some of the song fragments, which we have used until now for practising module technique, into a complete song so that you gradually build up your repertoire. Always bear in mind, that someone who can play just a dozen standards without printed music is able to play freely im-provised music for a good half hour at a party, or anywhere else. This should give you the necessary incentive to concentrate more intensively on developing your ear and the feeling of the chords in the hands and to break away more and more from simply reading music. Of course you will continue to read the examples presented, but only in order to work with them and to use your ear to make the chords, chord-modules, module sequences and passages your own.

Until now you have had only one com-plete song to play: 'Solitude'. But the beginnings of several songs have been hid-den in the different musical examples.

You will not be able to extend these song beginnings into whole songs immediate-ly as certain modules are still missing. But try to continue a song beginning as far as you can with the new modules you have learned. On page 68 you already encountered the first ten bars of the old song 'Just a Gigolo'.

We will now take the last two of those bars and add another two, which can be harmonized with the new module Gm^7 - A^9 - Dm^7.

Schöner Gigolo, armer Gigolo (Leonello Casucci/Julius Brammer)
© 1929 by Wiener Bohème Verlag GmbH, Berlin – München

Now try to repeat this song, with the additional bars, and learn to play it from memory. I do not know if you like the sound of the Gm^7 with the seventh interval in the bass. Before you memorize this passage, decide whether you prefer Gm^7 with the simple *g* in the bass. The seventh interval with a minor seventh chord is purely a matter of personal preference. If the bass note is low, as in the Cm^7 chord, you cannot use it as it does not sound good to have two notes so close together at such a low pitch.

We could actually play this melody right through to the end. We have already learn-

ed the module that we need next. But that would distract us from the Gm^6 - A^9 (or Gm^7 - A^9) module that we are dealing with just at the moment. This Cj^7 - Gm^6 - A^9 transition occurs in principle only when the melody note is either *g* or *e*. Of course the melody can move around this position by a semitone or a whole tone while the same chord sounds. Or the melody line might begin with the *g* or *e* in Cj^7 and rise or fall one or two steps over Gm^6 to A^9.

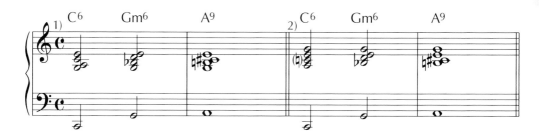

It might look like this if the melody moves around the starting note in semitone or whole-tone steps while the same chord sounds:

And finally, another two examples of this module with the melody either rising or falling through the chord progression.

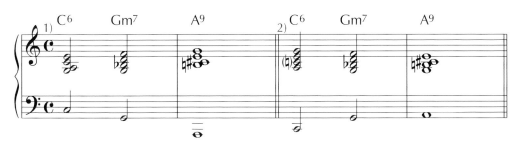

In the first example the bass goes down from *c* on the staff to low *a* beneath the staff. With the low *a* we must of course leave out the seventh interval so as not to produce an indefinable dissonance. This descending movement in the bass with an ascending melody is a very old musical practice, which is almost always observed in classical music. We have kept to it on this occasion, although in avant garde classical music, in modern classical music and also in jazz, this contrary motion of the bass, along with the required avoidance of fifths and parallel octaves, is not observed. Please excuse the rather contradictory term 'modern classical music'. I have this as the term 'classical' music is often used in a misleading way.

Now let us get back to our C^6 - Gm^6 - A^9 module. We now want to extend this with the end module G^9 - G^{9-} - C^6 so that it sounds elegant. To do this we add a kind of link between the two modules, i.e. D^9. D^9 is not altogether unfamiliar to you as it appeared in Duke Ellington's 'Solitude', in bar 12. Let us just take another look at it in its various positions:

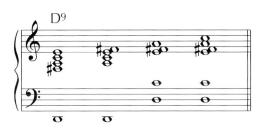

So, now add this D^9 to the C^6 - Gm^6 - A^9 module and listen carefully to the sounds. As well as this, try to find the easiest, most comfortable positions in which to play this succession of the four chords C^6 - Gm^6 - A^9 - D^9. We have chosen **e** as the melodic note as in this position all four chords, as well as the two that have been added on, can be played with this note. This is very effective in so-called fillers or links between musical phrases.

This new D^9 is like all ninth chords – as we have often mentioned – a seventh chord with a third like a little hat on top. The D seven chords are D^7, $D^{7/6}$, $D^{7/+}$, D^{9-} and the variant $D^{7/4}$. You could use the seventh interval in the bass for any of these. We did not do this in the previous example. The D^9 is at such a low pitch that it does not work. We also often left out this interval with the A^9 chords in the examples on the previous page. The seventh interval does not always need to be used. And if you do use it, it does not necessarily have to be played only by the left hand. You can play the **g** of A^9 with the thumb of the right hand. So it is up to you whether you use the seventh inverval or not. You will soon see from our musical examples that you cannot play this seventh interval when the chords are at a low pitch and that when the chord is pitched around the middle of the stave, the chord can sometimes be divided between the hands. When the chord is in a high position you could play the bass an octave higher, or an octave lower, depending on the sound you want at a particular point. I would like quickly to show you the last alternative before we continue our module-building.

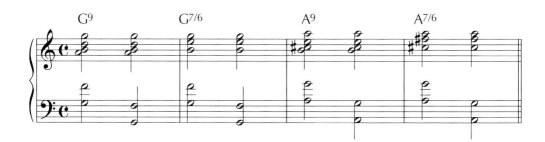

Now we will fulfil our intention of linking the C^6 - Gm^6 - A^9 module with the ending module G^9 - G^{9-} - C^6 (or C^{j7}) by inserting a D^9.

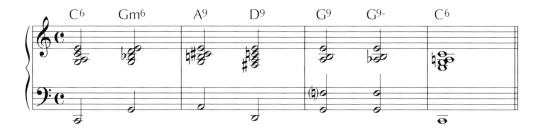

Please listen to this chain of sounds very intently. Spend some time working on this. Your fingers must get used to playing these chords before you can produce a really good sound.

At this point I would particularly like to draw to your attention the fact that the touch required for songs, hits and lyrical jazz ballads is not the same as the gently hammering classical touch, I mean the kind of touch that gives polyphonic baroque music the required precision. For chord progressions such as the one above we push the keys into the piano rather than hammering them. Of course pushing down the chords requires particularly fine ear control. These rather complicated chords must be depressed very evenly so that the sound is balanced. If only one of the notes produced is quieter than the others, the whole effect of the chord may be lost; or it may even produce a slight discord. There is a con-siderable amount of friction within our chord construction. The individual notes of a chord must be played in a particular position as they would produce an ab-solute discord if they were played arbitrarily in any position. If, for example, we 'dissect' the G^9 chord, we can hear immediately that three of the five elements – *f*, *g*, *a flat* – would produce a quite awful dissonance if you placed them right next to each other. The quite distinctive

9^- sound can only be achieved by placing the notes in a particular way and by playing the notes with absolute evenness of tone and volume.

You might have noticed that three ninth chords appeared in succession, A^9 - D^9 - G^9, with only the A^9 being announced by its herald. Of course an Am^7 chord could have been added before D^9 and Dm^7 be-fore G^9. But the succession was quicker and more direct without the heralds. We reached our goal more swiftly.

However, so that you do not forget the practice of playing heralds first, play the sequence from C⁶ to G⁹ once again, this time giving each chord its appropriate announcement.

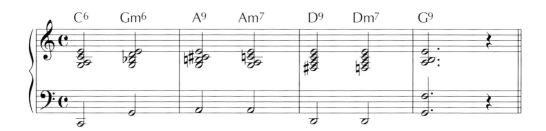

If there is a long succession of chords with the same melody note, the heralds do not always sound appropriate, as the melodic note is not always a part of the chord. For example, in the previous example with Dm^7, where the *e* in the melody does not fit. The Am^7 does not go very well with the melody note in this position as we had the same notes in the right hand just two beats earlier, only with a different bass note. So you will see that in using heralds in our chord constructions we must use our ear to keep control.

However, with a normal melody line that rises and falls there is a greater chance that a herald will fit in well. Let us take the end of the song 'Just a Gigolo', which we began on page 68 and continued on page 94.

Schöner Gigolo, armer Gigolo (Leonello Casucci/Julius Brammer)
© 1929 by Wiener Bohème Verlag GmbH, Berlin – München

Try to absorb this piece with your ear and practise it until you play it well. When you can do this, free yourself from the notation so that you can play it entirely from memory. With these chords we now have all the necessary components to tackle our second song. So that you don't have to keep on turning back, here is the complete song:

Schöner Gigolo, armer Gigolo (Leonello Casucci/Julius Brammer)
© 1929 by Wiener Bohème Verlag GmbH, Berlin – München

Please play this song very very slowly. Break it up into small sections. Take the first section and play it until you can play the chords well and you no longer have to look at the printed music. Only then should you go on to the next musical phrase. I am no doubt repeating myself, if I draw your attention to the fact that all the chord constructions in this song appear again in some other. This is why it is so important to work on memorizing a few songs to master freedom in your playing. You will be amazed later and pleased when you come across one chain of modules or another that is so familiar to your fingers and in your mind that you can play it through almost subconsciously right away. So I ask you to make the effort to do

99

this necessary work on memorizing now although you will not reap the benefits until later. We are dealing with an extensive and complex subject area that requires one virtue in particular to conquer: patience!

I can well imagine what you are going through at the moment and what you might be thinking. Everything that we have worked through so far has sounded very pleasantly harmonic. We have acquired a quite considerable collection of ingredients for our creations and really we now lack only a few exotic spices, which are by no means essential. So why does everything still sound rather boring? In spite of our eager culinary efforts, everything still tastes like a boring soup. Why is this? There is an essential ingredient missing from our mixture: rhythm. Without rhythm, standards and jazz cannot sound right.

Without rhythm there is no drive, no pepper. It does not carry you along. Even if we decorate our melodies with attractive chord modules, there still remains a rather dull and dreary feeling. And this is not surprising as in many places we are simply holding chords on for several bars without moving. That must appear boring.

For the time being, however, we must put aside the matter of all the tricks and techniques of rhythm. We must concentrate on one thing at a time if we want to avoid confusion. It is complicated enough to master all the strange chords, modules and sequences of modules. We need to continue to work on this persistently, step by step. We have already achieved a great deal.

So, to continue, we will now work on short melodies that we will set with chords; with sequences of modules that appear again and again. And so we can build on the beginnings of songs that we have already discussed and complete them or add one or another new song to our collection.

On page 67 we had a very beautiful melody. Let us take the last few bars and add on a sort of melodic section in which the change A^9 - D^9 appears.

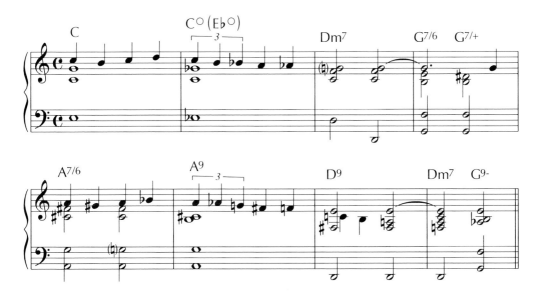

A Fine Romance (Jerome Kern/Dorothy Fields)
© 1936 by T. B. Harms Company, New York
Chappell & Co., Ltd., 50, New Bond Street, London W1 & Sydney

Then it continues with bar 1 of page 67. From bar 9 another melodic section is added, which we will deal with later and which will lead us on to the end of the piece.

Here we find the module $A^{7/6}$ - A^9 - D^9. We have not encountered $A^{7/6}$ before, but this chord is very simple and logical if you have already worked with the one which lies a tone lower, $G^{7/6}$, as we have.

Something else might have been new to you: with D^9 we have let the middle note of the C chord (in the right hand) descend by steps so that we do not have to hold on the same chord. Such a small transition, though not an exciting rhythmic enrichment, at least introduces some movement.

Let us continue to work with some short
melodic fragments with which we can use
the modules we have just learned.

I think that you will gradually be getting
used to playing the module chain C - E♭°
- Dm^7 - G$^{7/+}$. Your ear, too, will be more
familiar with these sounds. I mean the
pure harmonies, rather than the complete
sound including the melody. We want to
get used to the characteristic sound of a
particular chord whatever melody it
might be underlying.

So G$^{7/+}$, for example, is quite easy to pick
out of the chord progression with its
individual tone colour. I can imagine that
you are also already able to recognize the
melancholy sound of G^{9-}. It is more diffi-

cult, however, to identify a normal G^9, a
D^9 or an A^9 immediately by ear from a
chord progression. This requires a lot of
practice.

The next melodic line once again uses the
chain Gm - A^9 - D^9 - G^6, which we used
recently at a different pitch.

In the penultimate bar of this example there is a transition in which there is a momentary flash of a G^{9-} before coming to the final C^6 chord. This example needs to be played slowly so that the relatively fast chord changes of the transition can be fully appreciated.

Perhaps we should just mention the herald here. With A^9 until now we have used the second herald, the announcer that lies only one step below the following seventh chord (Gm^6 - A^9). Now we should also use the herald that lies 4 steps lower, Em^7. Here, too, we can make things easier for ourselves if we use the now familiar combination Dm^7 - G^9 (or $G^{7/6}$ or $G^{7/+}$) and push it up one step.

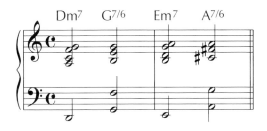

With D^9 the herald is Am^7.

While Gm^6 serves as second herald for A^9, the Gm^7 becomes the first precursor for C^9.

Please don't become agitated over the use of the terms 'first' herald and 'second' herald. You do not really need to think about this or take note of it. I simply want to point out that there is not just one precursor. In due course we will become familiar enough with these chord precursors, so we need not worry about calculating the number of steps up or down just at the moment. Whenever we discuss them, we shall only do so in connection with a particular example.

If you study the sound of the previous musical examples, you will notice once more how important it is to depress the piano keys evenly. Each individual note of a chord must reach the ear at the same volume. The first chord (Gm^6) and the fourth chord (C^9) are absolutely identical in the right hand. Only the bass differs and creates the contrast in sound. The third chord (Gm^7) is almost identical to the fourth (C^9). The difference lies only in one single note. If you happen to play this weaker than the others the harmonic statement will not be true.

It is just the same with the preceding examples with the different minor seventh chords. For those the right hand has to play five notes at once. If one of those is just a bit weaker, the sound is not complete and the ear hears a different sound to that intended.

Those of you who have always played classical music until now will be more used to the polyphonic style. The notes are played in more rapid succession, while the notes in our musical examples are usually played all at once. Later, however, when we come to the 'Rhythm' chapter we will look over to polyphony.

The composers and interpreters in the world of jazz are always so immensely proud of their complicated and tricky chords. They imagine that classical music is rather straightforward and simple with regard to chord structure. Many jazzers rack their brains day and night to try and make certain sounds even more complicated, trying to find chords that have not yet been discovered. And if one of them really thinks that he has succeeded in this, he must then realize to his shame that Johann Sebastian Bach had already used this chord three hundred years ago in one of his fugues, or that you can find it in the music of Claude Debussy.

CHAPTER 5

THE MERRY-GO-ROUND OF FIFTHS

The quickest and most elegant means of transport to cover the complete circuit of twelve keys is the Merry-Go-Round of Fifths; the seventh-chord Merry-Go-Round of Fifths. Using the seventh chords (^{7}, $^{7/6}$, $^{7/+}$, ^{9}, $^{9-}$, etc.) is the most direct way of going from one key to another. You could send out a herald to achieve a pleasant ornamentation of the sound, but when you are in a hurry, you can leave out the herald.

These journeys from one key to another are particularly appropriate in our kind of music. You have already experienced that we play songs in C major without a key signature, but that we bring in all kinds of foreign chords: F^6, D^9, A^9, Em^7, etc. And other related chords from different keys turn up.

Later we will even play complete songs in other keys. To then go from one song that is written, for example, in G major, to the next one in F major, we need to find a transition that leads the ear into the next key. The most powerful magnets of movement are of course the seventh chords, as they attract harmonies without fail to the major or minor key that lies five steps below (though in exceptional cases also to the minor key one step higher). So, for example, A^7 is drawn towards D major, D^7 towards G major.

The surprising thing is now, that – as you have already practised – you can follow a seventh chord immediately with the seventh chord that lies five steps lower without first landing on the corresponding major or major sixth chord. You have already come across this case in the example on page 96. There you travelled non-stop from A^9 to D^9 and from there immediately to G^9.

107

that jump from one key to another using sequences of seventh chords.

If you continue this chain reaction, always going to the seventh chord five steps lower, you will at some point come back to where you started. This is why we call it the Merry-Go-Round of Fifths.

Thankfully, there are no songs that make this world tour. There are, however, well-known melodies such as, for example, 'All the things you are' by Jerome Kern,

You can see from the number of chords that we have mastered so far that we have actually been very conscientious until now. We only need another two seventh chords, then we'll be able to ride more than half way round the Merry-Go-Round of Fifths. Let us begin one of these express rides immediately with the two new seventh chords, B^9 and E^9, from seventh chord to seventh chord.

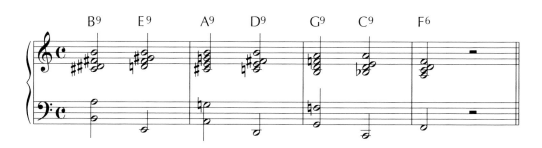

In one stroke we have passed through six keys and have landed on the seventh, and in only a few bars of music. Only seventh chords can achieve such a speedy result.

Now let us look at one of these chords more closely: the B^9 chord. B^9 has a certain similarity to $C°$, both in construction and in sound.

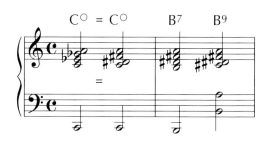

Apart from the bass, there is only one different note in the two chords, that is the lowest note in the right hand: a *c* in the C° chord and *c sharp* in the B^9 chord.

The B^9 chord does not often appear in songs in C major. So it is not necessary to introduce all the inversions and related seventh forms (B^7, $B^{7/4}$, $B^{7/+}$, B^{9-}, etc.) in a table. We will simply add it to some of our melodic passages. This is the quickest way to get to know it. There is a lovely American standard that is typical in its use of the B^9 chord. The song is called 'Whispering'.

Another complete song! An old-fashioned foxtrot in which we unfortunately have several bars with the same chord held for a whole bar. We will not be in a position to address this lack of rhythmic interest until later. At the moment we must put up with this tedium. In the two bars with the chord symbol A^9 we have tried, in a simple way, to relieve the monotony. Instead of holding the chords on for four beats, one of the notes of the chord has been moved around so that one note sounds on each beat. This is the most primitive way of bringing a bit of rhythm into a chord – but better than nothing.

Following on from the new module C - B^9 we meet the module chain A^9 - D^9 - Dm^7 - G^9, with which we are already very familiar. This chain will in future appear so often that we will soon be able to play it in our sleep.

Please do not worry if you see a seventh interval (in the bass) with a particular seventh or minor seventh chord that did not have the seventh interval in earlier examples, or if there is no seventh interval where there was one before. First of all, you can choose to play whatever you like. Secondly, it also depends very much on the pitch of the chord at a particular moment, so that you would automatically avoid a seventh interval if the notes of the right hand are too low.

As B^9 is rather remote from C major, and carries with it a whole backpack full of sharp signs, the module C - B^9 is often replaced by the rather similar-sounding module C - $E\flat°$ in the harmonization of melodies. In the next two systems of music the same melody is shown first with one combination, then with the other. Your ear will establish that there is no great difference in the sound.

A chord of much more importance than B^9, is the chord E^9 – the second new chord in our Merry-Go-Round of Fifths from page 108. This chord appears in many, many songs and with this we have, in principle, the last chord-element we need to play conventional standards in C major. Of course we will not make do with this collection of chords. In the next two chapters we will move on to more sophisticated sounds. Before that, though, we want to work the E^9 chord into a whole series of melodies. We will also complete three more melodies so that our repertoire will consist of six pieces.

On the Sunny Side of the Street (Jimmy McHugh/Dorothy Fields)

That is the beginning of the standard 'On the Sunny Side of the Street' by Jimmy McHugh. You have probably heard this melody before. Instead of the E^9 chord, we could have used $E^{7/6}$.

$E^{7/6}$ actually sounds just as good as E^9 and is much easier to play, though this applies only when the melody note is at this pitch.

In the last bar of the example about (G^9 - $B°$) we made a further attempt at introducing rhythm by bringing in at least one note on each beat of the bar. This time we did not just pick a note of the chord and move it around. We simply 'forgot' to play one note of the G^9 chord on the first beat and held it back until the second beat. This is really nothing wonderful and yet it already helps to relieve the tedium of the long, sustained chords.

Now let us get back to our E^9 chord. As we will use this much more often than B^9, we should take a look at all its inversions:

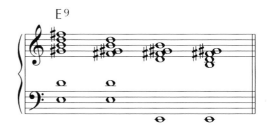

The first two inversions can of course be played an octave lower.

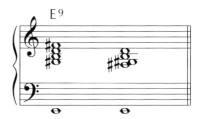

Here we have another case where the seventh interval cannot be used in the bass. We will now add on the next few bars of 'On the Sunny Side of the Street' as this introduces the lowest of these two E^9 chords, though only for one crotchet beat.

Slowly

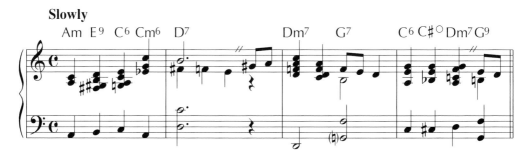

This is a rather interesting harmonization, isn't it? A complicated chord sequence like this requires a lot of practice. In this respect you should bear in mind that this book is not a novel that can be read through quickly and then put aside. You could spend several days on a few bars like this for your fingers really to become familiar with the notes and for your ear to get used to the sounds.

In the last bar, the melody begins with a *g*. Really this *g* should be held on for three crotchet beats. Again, this would be rather tedious. To avoid this, this time we are not going to use the surrounding notes, neither do we delay playing one of the components of the chord. We have simply built in a filler. While the singer would hold on the melody note for three beats at this point, we play a different chord on each beat: C^6 - $C\#^\circ$ - Dm^7.

With this we have created a new module that makes a great filler – a good way of avoiding tedium on the melody note *g*. Let us take this module and have a good look at it, as this final bar with a long sustained *g* appears at the end of many musical phrases.

There is just one symbol here that we have not encountered before: $C\#^\circ$. But we have already played the chord.

$C\#^\circ = D\flat^\circ$

As with all three diminished chords, any of the four notes can appear in the bass. So you will encounter it under four different names. Actually, even five, as instead of $C\#^\circ$ it can also be called $D\flat^\circ$: $C\#^\circ$, $D\flat^\circ$, E°, G° and $B\flat^\circ$. Please learn the filler-module C^6 - $C\#^\circ$ - Dm^7 - $G^{7/6}$ from memory. It is useful in many passages. Now let us get back to E^9.

Anyone who likes doing crossword puzzles will know that the letter E comes up most often. With songs in the key of C, the note **g** is used most often in the melody. Of course a melody often goes up or down a semitone and you will see the series of notes **g** - **g sharp** - **a** again and again.

There are many chords with which we can harmonize a **g** or an **a** in the melody. But there are not many that sound too good with a **g sharp**. Here the E⁹ proves to be an ideal partner in melodies that are in C major.

The 'Charleston' begins with the notes **g** - **g sharp** - **a** in the melody.

So there are many songs which begin with such a melodic figure, without even mentioning those in which the **g - g sharp - a** appear during the course of the song. Very often, the E^9 sets in motion the Merry-Go-Round of Fifths so that the A^9, D^9 and G^9 follow, as in the Charleston.

In the example the seventh intervals in the bass are interesting. We always place these intervals at as high a pitch as possible, as close as possible to the rest of the chord. You can see this quite clearly in the penultimate bar, in which the melody rises to a higher pitch.

I think that using C^6 as the first chord will not have bothered you. It is just one of the possible variants when we do not want to use the straight C major chord, which sounds rather ordinary. Your ear will have

now become accustomed to more complicated chords. I hope that these chords are not painful to your ear, as might have been the case in the beginning, if you are used to the pure sounds of classical music.

Of course the E^9 chord does not only occur with a semitone step from **g sharp** to **a**. You will find it in many other situations. If we were to continue the melody found on page 61, for example, we would find this chord. It appears after an F - F#°- C sequence that is followed by the sequence Am - D^9 - Dm^7 - $G^{7/6}$ - G^9.

We will now notate the whole song, rather than just this section, to extend your repertoire. The song is called 'Penthouse Serenade'.

Penthouse Serenade (Will Jason/Val Burton)
© 1931 by Famous Music Corp., 1619 Broadway, New York, N. Y.

We need to talk in detail about the construction of this song as there are a few chords that appear in a rather unusual form. Our knowledge of chords should be extended with each new encounter, but this should never lead to confusion. Anyone who is exploring the art of play-ing the piano freely will at first automatically make use of complete chords. If you see the symbol Dm^7, for example, you would expect – at least in some order – the components d - f - a - c in order to complete the chord in the familiar way. A chord immediately looks quite different, even unfamiliar, if one of its components is missing.

As we are aiming to free ourselves more and more from the restrictions of pure note-reading, it remains for us to construct the chords ourselves from the symbols given, at whatever pitch suits the melody. Of course it would be preferable if we always had to use the complete chord. Then there would be no exceptions or alternatives. How can we know when to leave out a note of the chord and when not to? And which of the four or five notes should be left out? What are the rules we can apply?

There aren't any! We are not obliged to play in a certain way – unlike when we play from printed music. Then you must play what is written! Everything that is written! And nothing but what is written!

So, if you wish, and if it is possible, you can play every note of the chord. I said if it is possible. As we now give the first reason why we might be forced to leave out one note of a chord.

Let us take, for example, G^9, which frequently appears in our melodies. It consists of the notes *g*, *b*, *d*, *f* and *a*, which can in most cases all be used. If, however, the melody note is the low *c* (**middle c**), which happens now and then, we cannot possibly use the *b* of the chord.

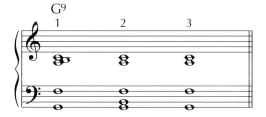

It does not go in the right hand (1), because then there would be three notes right next to each other (**a**, **b**, **c**), which would sound awful. It sounds just as bad if you put the **b** in the bass a third above the key note (2). We are therefore forced to simply leave out the **b** (3). You will notice that in spite of this the G^9 has lost none of its charm.

The decision as to whether we include or leave out a note of a chord is made by our ear. If you close your eyes and ask your ear the question, you will always receive an answer. You will immediately recognize in which form the chord produces the best sound.

There is another circumstance in which you may be forced to exclude one note of a chord. That is when the chord would be too difficult to play when the melody is at a certain pitch. This often happens when the melody is at a rather fast tempo. You then simply do not have time to move from one chord to all the notes of the next one if there is a difficult change in the hand position. Here, too, there is only one way out; that is, to omit one of the notes.

Your ear will often decide that one chord or another sounds just as good in a certain position despite a missing note, and it will be much easier to play. Why should you create difficulties for yourself if the result is no more satisfying?

I know exactly that all this reflection will trouble you. You will no doubt say: how on earth can I quickly take this into consideration during the course of a song? There is no time for all this!

That is right! To be able to play a song fluently, the individual chords must be quite free from calculation and completely embedded in your subconscious. Then they will be at your fingertips, immediately and without having to think.

To this end we will examine several musical examples. Let us begin with the normal C major chords. How can we alter the dull, unexciting *c* - *e* - *g* chord, and when is it appropriate to leave out one of the elements of the chord?

First of all, we can establish that it is always fine to use the simple *c* - *e* - *g* chord if the melody note is not one of these, for example, *a*, *b*, *d*.

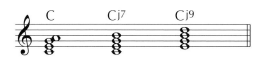

Of course it then becomes a C⁶, Cʲ⁷ or Cʲ⁹. This will not necessarily be indicated in the chord symbol.

And now let us look at the possible deviations from the normal C major chord when we take the *c* an octave above **middle c**. In this position we can use C⁶ without any problems without having to omit a note.

To produce a Cʲ⁷ sound in this position you could add a *b* to the *e* - *g* - *c* structure. This would, however, create a rather strange sound.

It is different if you want to produce a Cʲ⁹ in this position. This is no problem at all: but only if you throw out one note of this chord, i.e. the *b*.

Take a good look at this chord! Get used to playing it so that you do not need to work it out when you come to use it.

When the melody note *c* is in this position you can therefore replace the boring C chord with two more interesting chords:

1. with C^6 (complete chord)

2. with C^{j9} (incomplete chord)

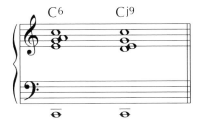

Now let us look at the replacement possibilities for the ordinary C chord when the note *g* is at the top. In this position you can make use of all three variants without losing a note: C^6, C^{j7} and C^{j9}, though the last one sounds rather unusual and would sound best if used as a final chord. So we will keep to the C^6 and C^{j7} chords, both in their complete form.

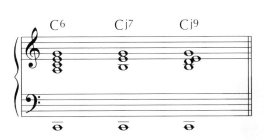

Now we are left with the replacement chords in the position with *e* as the melody note. Here, too, all three possibilities can be used without any losses: C^6, C^{j7} and C^{j9}, which again sounds rather odd.

If we use the 'Penthouse Serenade' as a test run for the chords that are being absorbed into our subconsciousness, the first two systems should bring into effect a well-known pattern of chord changes, as we are familiar with the C - $Eb°$ module in this position;

as well as the chord progression Dm^7 - $G^{7/6}$.

You will also be quite used to playing Dm^7 with the *g* at the top although this is a very complicated chord.

If, however, we take a closer look at the G$^{7/6}$ in the fourth bar and the G^9 in the fifth bar, it becomes absolutely obvious that something is missing from both chords, that is, the note *d*. They are therefore incomplete chords that we have known for some time, and the G$^{7/6}$ is also such a chord.

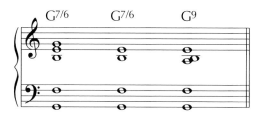

In the seventh bar of 'Penthouse Serenade' the module C - E♭° appears once again. Here it jumps from one chord to the other – one octave higher. As the right-hand *c* is so low, we have omitted the usual doubling of the *c*. The E♭° chord is complete this time. In this module we have until now left out the *a* of its components *c - e flat - g flat (=f sharp) - a*; unless, of course, it occurred in the melody. But please feel free to use the module C - E♭° in future in its complete form – as we have here.

The middle section of the song now follows (the last eight bars of our musical example), which is completely new to us. First of all we move into F major by means of the C^9 chord and its herald Gm^7. Many middle sections (so-called 'bridges') of standards in C major begin with an excursion to F major.

A middle section always consists of eight bars and provides a great contrast to the main motive of the song. The theme, or main motive, also consists of eight bars. It is usually played twice in succession before going on to the middle section. To finish, the eight bars of the theme appear once again.

For songs in C major that have such a middle section, the following 32-bar structure is produced:

1. Theme (8 bars), last chord is G^7 (or variant) as a transition to the repetition of the theme.

2. Theme (8 bars), same melody as 1. but with C as the final chord.

3. Middle section (8 bars), completely different melody, completely different chords, last chord is usually G^7 to lead back to the theme.

4. Theme (8 bars), same melody as 2.

There are, however, many standards, such as, for example, George Gershwin's 'But Not For Me' or 'I Can't Give You Anything But Love' by Jimmy McHugh, that have no middle section. Their theme is 16 bars long and is repeated, so that these songs too usually have 32 bars.

The middle section of 'Penthouse Serenade' is typical of most 'bridges'. The melody progresses in sequences. The chords change over first to F major and then go back to C. The rest of the course proceeds by means of the Merry-Go-Round of Fifths E^9 - Am - D^9 - (Dm^7) $G^{7/6}$.

You must learn the Gm^7 - C^9 - F module, whether you spread out the F chord or play the notes all at once as F^6 or F^{j7} like this:

The module C - E^9 - Am follows on from this. You will come across this again and again in different positions. With the Am chord we practise our passing notes: one of the notes of the chord (the **a**) can be moved downwards in semitone steps, so that nobody will fall asleep.

Do not be irritated by the Am station on this ride on the Merry-Go-Round of Fifths. It does not necessarily have to be E^9 - A^9 - D^9 - G^9. The Am chord can be used just as well as A^9.

The D^9 chord in the fourth bar from the end is incomplete: the **a** is missing so that we can play the melody more easily. You could play the complete chord if you wish, if the melody line would not be too difficult for you to play. The last two bars will be familiar to you, although the final G^9 chord is incomplete. If you compare the sound of the complete chord played at this pitch with the incomplete one, you will agree with me that it is really not worth playing too many notes. The typical G^9 sound is still present in the incomplete form.

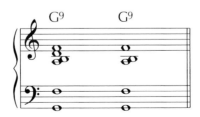

So, we have ploughed through 'Penthouse Serenade'. In the end it is up to you whether you play the chords in their complete form or not. You need only

to be certain when a simple chord is preferable to the complete chord, as later you will be playing songs at a faster tempo in which chords that are complicated to play will be troublesome.

It will do no harm to take a quick look at one or two typical middle sections. I mean bridges, like the one in 'Penthouse Serenade', which first change over to F major and then have a short section travelling around the Merry-Go-Round of Fifths, usually only from D^9 - G^9.

This bridge construction is one of the forms most commonly used in popular songs. The harmonic course of many bridge passages begins with Gm^7 - C^9 - Fj^9, followed by the module chain Am^7 - D^9 - Dm^7 - G^9.

The well-known standard 'On the Sunny Side of the Street' by Jimmy McHugh has a bridge passage constructed in this way. It would be best now to look at the complete song. You can take a closer look at the bridge passage.

On the Sunny Side of the Street (Jimmy McHugh/Dorothy Fields)
© 1930 by Shapiro, Bernstein & Co., Inc., New York, N. Y.
© renewed 1957. Für Deutschland, Österreich, Bulgarien,
Ungarn, Jugoslawien, Polen, CSFR, Rumänien, Albanien:
MELODIE DER WELT, J. Michel KG, Musikverlag, Frankfurt/Main

With this song, our repertoire consists of five songs already. You should play through them a few times every day to get used to them. 'On the Sunny Side of the Street' should be played quite slowly to begin with as there is a different chord on almost every note of the melody. From this point of view, it is rather a difficult song. On the other hand, it contains all the traditional elements in different positions, as the melody is constantly rising and falling. If you can learn to play this melody without looking at the printed music this will be a great achievement.

You will have noticed that we have made modest attempts to add rhythmic interest in places. For the time being it will suffice to repeat a chord rather than simply holding it on for a long time, as, for example, in the fourth and sixth bars. Incomplete chords can also be rearranged. These chords cannot be played in their complete form as the pitch of the melody is too low. We have not played a complete chord at this pitch until the very last C^6 chord of the song. Why this one and not the others? Well, this is the final chord, which you would always like to sound as full as possible. Apart from this, there is no need to hurry as, once it has been played, there is nothing to follow. So we do not need to simplify it.

Unfortunately there are no great rides on the Merry-Go-Round of Fifths in this song. As the Merry-Go-Round of Fifths is supposed to be the main theme of this chapter, we should examine a few more examples. First let us look at the middle section of the old American hit 'Everywhere You Go'. Here is a completely smooth ride on the Merry-Go-Round of Fifths from E^9 to G^9, a journey without any delays or detours: E^9 - A^9 - D^9 - G^9. Listen to this lovely melodic passage:

Everywhere You Go (Larry Shay/Mark Fisher)
© 1927 Copyright renewed 1949 by Lombardo Music Inc., 1619 Broadway, New York, N. Y.

In the fourth bar we have added interest by repeating the inner notes of the chord.

Gradually we are becoming accustomed to this simple technique.

Here is another example in which we travel from B major (B^9) to C major by means of fifths.

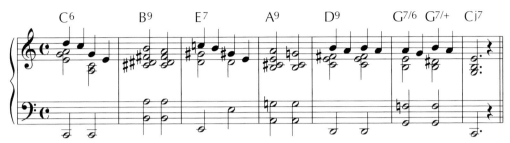

If you look away from the B^9 chord for a moment, we are dealing with chords that are rather rare in the Merry-Go-Round of Fifths found in standards in the key of C major: E^9, A^9 and D^9. Instead of A^9 or D^9 you could play $A^{7/6}$ and $D^{7/6}$. The E, A and D chords are also in different positions, so it is not easy to get used to playing them. Modules such as this, which are dictated by the Merry-Go-Round of Fifths, are found in most standards. We will therefore have plenty of opportunities to use them. Nevertheless, we should begin to get used to a few of them, first of all those in the most frequently used positions.

Harmonize the following melody with the chords indicated in the symbols.

The first chord is quite straightforward. Play a low **c** in the bass, that is fixed, and in the right hand play the C major chord, **c** - **e** - **g**, with the sixth step, **a**, added. It cannot be added at the top as we cannot add notes above the melody. It must therefore go below the **c**.

Next comes the E^7 chord. If we play the seventh interval in the bass (**e** - **d**), there is only space in this position for the right hand to play one more note, that is the **e**. So we could not play an E^9 chord here, but simply the E^7. If the E^9 symbol had been given, we would have played a low **e** in the bass rather than the seventh interval to make space in the right hand for all the notes of the E^9 chord.

The $A^{7/6}$ does not present any problems if we take our old familiar $G^{7/6}$ and transpose it up a tone.

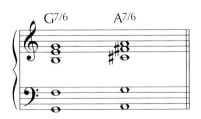

The last remaining chord is D^9 in the C position, that is, with the note *c* in the melody. Here we have enough space to play the seventh interval in the bass and still fit in all the elements of D^9 in the right hand: *d - f sharp - a - c - e*. The *d* and *c* are already in the bass. We will therefore add an *a*, *f sharp*, and *e* beneath the *c* of the melody. The chord is then complete. Try playing it without the *a* and let your ear decide whether you can leave this note out or not. I think you can!

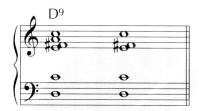

So now that we have worked carefully through this passage, let us look at the complete progression.

With the C^6 chord in the example above you could easily have played the *c* in the bass an octave higher, so that the interval in the left hand would not have been so great.

As we will be using the chords of E^9, $A^{7/6}$ and D^9 frequently in the forthcoming examples, we should try to get used to playing them in their most common positions.

What do we need to do to replace the rather boring E^7 of the last musical example with an E^9 chord? It is quite simple: instead of playing the seventh interval in the bass, play just a low *e*. Then we have space to play all the elements of E^9 in the right hand.

With the notes *e* - *b* - *d* of the E^9 chord we can harmonize four melody notes, from *d* to *g*. Take note of the foundation of the E^9 harmonization.

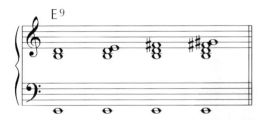

If, however, we take the seventh interval in the bass and the notes *f sharp* and *g sharp* in the right hand as a basis, we are able to harmonize higher melody notes with E^9.

![E9 (Basis) musical notation]

As D^9 is a whole tone lower than E^9, it follows that the D^9 basis is a whole tone lower than that of E^9 in the harmonization of a melody at a similar pitch.

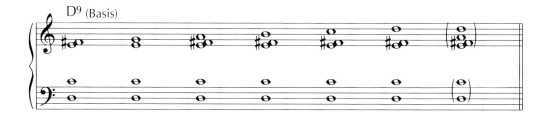

If you now want to set a melody around this pitch with E^9 - A$^{7/6}$ - D^6, it should not be too difficult to use the basic shape. For example, with the following melody line.

The first bars are quite easy to harmonize. Play the E^9 seventh interval **e - d** in the bass and in the right hand, apart from the melody note, the two foundation notes **f sharp** and **g sharp**. Then play A$^{7/6}$. The whole thing is repeated one tone lower in the following bars. The melody is quite similar to that on page 124. But now you have to make up your own chords. The result will be something like this:

I think that we are now more familiar with the E⁹, A⁷ᐟ⁶ and D⁹ chords. Memorize the characteristic shape of the E⁹ chord to use when the melody is at a higher pitch: the 7th interval in the bass; *f sharp* and *g sharp* in the right hand.

Let us take another quick look at the basic shape of the E⁹ and D⁹ chords for a low-pitched melody.

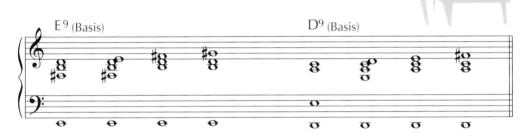

To form a ninth chord, the ninth step of the scale must appear somewhere beneath the melody note. In the E⁹ chord, this is *f sharp*, in D⁹ it is *e*. If the melody note is at a very low pitch, as in the first chord of this example, the ninth step can be placed a ninth above the bass note and you might be able to play the ninth interval in the left hand. If this is too uncomfortable, take the ninth into the right hand, and leave out one note of the chord.

You are, however, free to choose whether to play the whole chord or not.

It depends to a certain extent on the instrument, whether such a compact chord sounds good at a low pitch.

So the chords E^9 - A^9 (or $A^{7/6}$) - D^9 are very important when the Merry-Go-Round of Fifths is used in a C major standard. You have seen them now in a variety of positions, which may be a little confusing. Sometimes they have been complete, sometimes one note or another has been omitted. In most cases the complete sound would have been ideal. Unfortunately, there is not always time or space to play them all. To remove the need for decision-making, you are encouraged to play certain chords in the same way at a particular pitch. In time you will get used to these chord shapes. So, for example, when the melody note is E, $E^{7/6}$ is more practical than E^9.

Besides, you can create a great filler with the Merry-Go-Round of Fifths module $E^{7/6}$ - A^9 - D^9 - G^7 with the melody note *e*.

Please memorize this chord progression! Combinations such as this are always useful to have up your sleeve. They sound good and are relatively easy to play.

You will often find that the Merry-Go-Round of Fifths chords send out their own heralds. I would like to show you this before you come across it in later examples: Bm^7 - $E^{7/6}$ - Em^7 - $A^{7/6}$ - Am^7 - $D^{7/6}$ - Dm^7 - $G^{7/6}$.

Here we have some rather strange chords, yet they are quite practical to play. Melodies that are enriched with such sounds are much more interesting than those with primitive major and seventh chords.

With the low bass notes we have omitted the seventh interval to avoid producing a bass sound that cannot easily be distinguished by the ear and that is experienced by some people as a kind of buzzing.

Now we will gradually take our leave from the Merry-Go-Round of Fifths chapter. There is a lot of work in this important section, which has introduced many indispensable examples, examples that you should ideally memorize. This of course takes considerable time and so you should not move on from the pages of this chapter too quickly.

To finish with, we will now complete a song of which we already know the greater part. This is the song given on pages 67 and 101. It has 32 bars, but no bridge. It consists therefore of two 16-bar sections and is called 'A Fine Romance'. The melody is by Jerome Kern. The words were written by Dorothy Fields, who also wrote the text of Jimmy McHugh's 'On the Sunny Side of the Street'.

In this song we have left most of the chords that are held on for a whole bar without worrying about any lack of interest. Only in the third bar from the end have we introduced a transition that anticipates our later chapter on rhythm.

Please look closely at the individual chords, modules and module chains, study them and learn to play this melody gradually, until you do not need the printed music.

A Fine Romance (Jerome Kern/Dorothy Fields)
© 1936 by T. B. Harms Company, New York
Chappell & Co., Ltd., 50, New Bond Street, London W1 &
Sydney

132

CHAPTER 6

EXOTIC SOUNDS

We need to learn only five more chords to be able to play any standard in C major and many other keys. These five are exotic chords that are found in some songs, here and there, appearing out of the jungle of sounds, making a beautiful sound, and then disappearing again without trace. What makes them particularly attractive is their habit of not sending out a herald. You know that heralds sound rather good, but there is always a tendency to play them quickly, before the target chord. Minor seventh heralds must be played as complete chords and so they are rather complicated.

So it is very pleasant that our five exotic chords do not bring along any undesirable escorts. Such exotic creatures never appear with others of an exotic nature. They always dance alone out of the jungle of sound and disappear again immediately. Another of their lovable characteristics is that these chords are always relatively uncomplicated to play. They have no need

to contort themselves to sound as interesting as they are.

Having heard so much praise about these likable outsiders, we now want to try and entice one of them out of the jungle. One of these exotic chords would be very effective to use in a filler, at one of those rather tedious places where a melody note is held on for a whole bar or longer.

You probably guessed immediately that the second chord, the $E\flat^9$ was the exotic one. The key of Eb major is three stations away from C major in the Merry-Go-Round of Fifths and the chords of this key are very rarely seen in our realm; and then only sporadically.

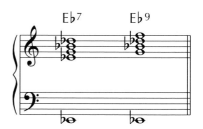

$E\flat^9$ appears in fillers but very rarely apart from this in songs in the key of C major. Let's take a look at another filler with $E\flat^9$. This filler is rather a tricky one as no sooner than one exotic chord has disappeared, another one comes along to commend itself.

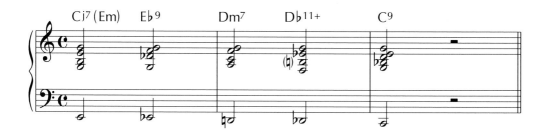

The $E\flat^9$ chord appears here in a slightly different form, but is just as easy to play as before. This is followed by the Dm^7 chord, which you have known for a long time and with which your fingers are no doubt very familiar.

Finally we come across another exotic chord ... an extremely exotic specimen. It comes from the family of D flat major and is very rarely seen in C major. With this chord we encounter the chord symbol 11+ for the first time. According to this it is a Db^9 with another major third on top. As there is a *g* in the melody here, the symbol Db^9 could just as well have been given; the melody note does not have to be indicated in the symbol. I just wanted to show you that eleventh chords do actually exist. They occur usually only in complicated jazz arrangements or in bossa novas. The $Db11^+$ chord is also a very unusual chord with regard to the hand position, as the right hand stretches over an octave – an interval of a ninth. This is of course a problem if you have small hands. In this case the chord could be rearranged like this:

It is clear that the components of such strange chords should be spread out as far as possible, as the closer the dissonances are to each other, the stronger the effect of the subliminal discord. The use of exotic chords is similar to the use of exotic spices. They are only desirable in precisely measured doses.

The filler module C - Eb^9 - Dm^7 - Db^{11+} - C^9 is one of the richest combinations of sound. If you learn it by the chord shapes, you will have at your fingertips elements for variations and transitions. The two exotic chords that have infiltrated, Eb^9 and Db^{11+} are very rare creatures in melodies in C major. It is therefore not necessary to give a theoretical commentary on their construction. Simply learn to play the previous examples from memory. Then you will have these exotic chords at your disposal, in case you should need them.

Now we come to the third exotic chord: Ab^9. In contrast to the two already mentioned, this outsider has a certain affinity with C major. The Hawaiians have taken to the C - Ab^9 chord change and use it to great effect in their beautiful folk music.

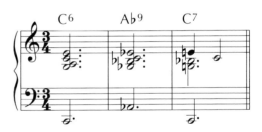

A lovely chord progression, isn't it? You can hear clearly that the chords C and Ab^9 go together very well. There seems to be some kind of congeniality between them. When a honey-yellow moon shines on the heavenly shore of an Hawaiian island and the hula-hula dancers decorated with beautiful flowers sing the wonderful chord progressions of their songs in perfect harmony, accompanied by ukeleles and Hawaiian guitars, you almost always hear this exotic chord at the end of their song:

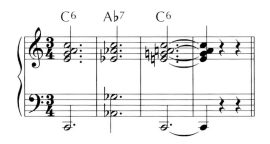

The A♭ chord does not only appear in fillers or in the final module of a song. It is found elsewhere in melodies in C major, for example in 'Bye Bye Blues':

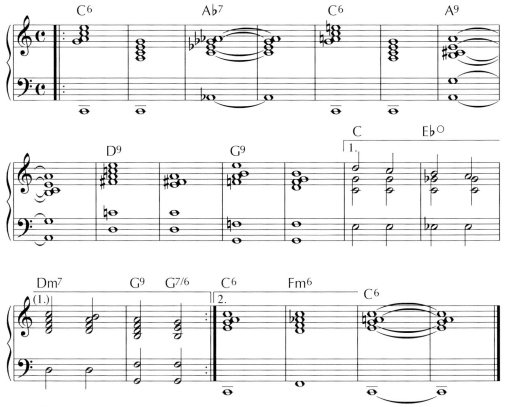

Bye Bye Blues (Fred Hamm/Dave Bennett/Bert Lown/Chauncey Grey)
© 1930 by Bourne Inc. New York, N. Y.
Für D-A-CH: Melodie der Welt, J. Michel KG, Musikverlag,
Frankfurt, Main

We shall not worry for the time being that this song consists predominantly of rather boring chords – that is, chords that are held on for four beats. We are concerned here with chord shapes in the right hand, which are very important for our training. We will deal later with introducing a bit more movement to the bass line and exploring ways of adding interest in the way chords are played.

The A♭ chord is found rather more frequently in standards than the other exotic chords, so we will look at it in a few typical situations.

As the change from a C major chord to an A♭ chord sounds interesting enough as it is, it is not absolutely necessary to play the A♭ chord as a ninth or $^{7/6}$ chord. An A♭^{6} or even an A♭^{7} would suffice to produce this exotic touch.

In discussing the E^7 chord we established that the melodic progression *g - g sharp - a* occurs quite frequently (see page 114) and that it is easy to harmonize the *g* and the *a*, but rather more difficult to find a chord for the *g sharp*.

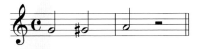

Well, here the A♭ chord is particularly useful as *a flat* and *g sharp* are the same note. You could therefore harmonize the melodic note *g* with C^6, the *g sharp* (*a flat*) with $A♭^7$ and the *a* with D^7, which might later lead to a G^9. Many songs begin like this, such as, for example, 'Poor Butterfly' by Raymond Hubbell.

Poor Butterfly (John Gold/Raymond Hubbell)
© 1916 (renewed) WARNER BROS INC.

Not all standards that begin with the melodic figure *g* - *g sharp* - *a* use the A♭ or E^9 chords to harmonize the *g sharp*. Some songs simply use C^+:

A typical example of this is the Harry Lime theme (from the film 'The Third Man') by Anton Karas. The melody constantly moves around the notes *g* - *g sharp* - *a*.

The C^+ is not indicated here as the $^+$ (the raised fifth step) appears really only as a passing note and a normal C chord follows immediately, although there is an *a* in the melody, which could be indicated by the symbol C^6.

There are some songs that begin with this melodic pattern with no chord at all. The indication 'tacet' should then be given or n.c. (no chord). An example of this is the French chanson 'Sous les toits de Paris' by Raoul Moretti. Here there is no chord for the upbeat **g** - **g sharp** of the melody.

Tempo di valse moderato

Sous les toits de Paris (Raoul Moretti)

The three melody notes **g** - **g sharp** (**a flat**) - **a** can also appear in the reverse order. In this case the **g sharp** is almost always harmonized with A♭:

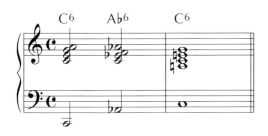

The exotic A♭ chord often appears after a C chord with an **e** in the melody.

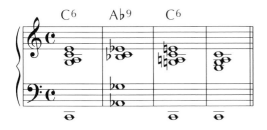

This is a typical passage in various Hawaiian songs. I like to use these Hawaiian songs as examples as these old folk melodies best reveal the amazing effect of this chord. The lead instrument used by the Hawaiians – the Hawaiian guitar – produces such a perfect fusion of melody and harmony that the great significance of the chord progression becomes clear. On this instrument the chord is usually struck one tone below the target key and then brought up to pitch, creating a certain tension. You can anticipate the chord before it is reached. The appreciation of the chord is then even greater when the final sound is achieved.

All these beautiful chords that we have learned so far are used by the Hawaiians simply, rationally, but to great effect. This is quite unusual in folk music, as folk melodies throughout the world often use the basic chord (for example, C), the appropriate seventh chord (G[7]) and the chord on the fourth step (F). Admittedly, there are wonderful Scottish, Irish, French, Italian, Spanish, Portuguese, Slav, Scandinavian, Japanese and other folk songs. But the Hawaiian folk songs are the most colourful in the world.

Another exotic chord favoured by the Hawaiians is F⁷. It sounds good in a C major passage and is simple to play.

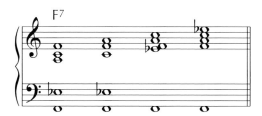

If F^9 is indicated in the chord symbols, we must add a *g* somewhere, as *g* is the ninth step of the F major scale. If the notes of the chord are too close together and the *g* cannot be forced in, leave out the note of the chord that is closest to the *g*.

The beautiful Hawaiian chord progressions can be seen best in the song 'Blue Hawaii' by Ralph Rainger and Leo Robin, which is a sensitive interpretation of an Hawaiian folk song. We will look at a few bars of this standard.

Blue Hawaii (Leo Robin/Ralph Rainger)
© 1936 and 1937 by Famous Music Corporation.
© renewed 1963 and 1964 by Famous Music Corporation

Here the normal seventh chord is good enough as the chords follow each other in quick succession and the effect is therefore quite colourful: C - C^7 - F^7 - C - Gm^6 - A^7 - D^9 - G^7 - C. At the end of this standard the F^7 chord is used rather than $A\flat^7$ as this is often used as the penultimate chord in Hawaiian songs. The last three chords of 'Blue Hawaii' accordingly look like this:

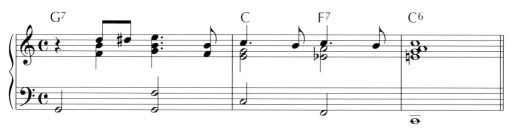

The F^7 chord is already the fourth of the five exotic chords announced to make an appearance in our show. The fifth is called $B\flat^7$. It hardly ever appears in Hawaiian songs played in the key of C major and also very rarely in standards in this key. It is used mainly by composers to achieve an unusual sound in certain places. This chord is added where another, normal, chord would usually be used. The whole thing then sounds rather strange and it is very rare that you will encounter this chord and feel that it really fits in. I would like to show you a passage from Henri Mancini's 'Moon River' where it appears briefly. This chord can under no circumstances be extended within a C major melody – it is always only a quick flash.

Even Duke Ellington, who uses some of the most unusual chord combinations, hardly ever uses it. And when he does use this chord, as in 'Mood Indigo', then it is only in a chord progression in which the ear actually wants to hear this sound. This shows the great insight and great talent of this amazing composer.

I have transposed this part of the song 'Mood Indigo', which is written in A flat major, into C major as we are used to this key at the moment and we have studied all the chord changes until now in relation to C.

Mood Indigo (Duke Ellington/Irving Mills/Albany Bigard)
© 1931 by MILLS MUSIC, Inc., New York, N. Y.

That is enough examples of the unusual appearance of the Bb7 or Bb9 chord within a C major passage. This chord appears much more often in songs in other keys. In Eb major it even plays a leading role, like the G7 in C major. If you work in this key later, at least you have already encountered it.

I would like briefly to come back to the Ab9 chord and, indeed, show it in a particular passage. It is the beginning of the song 'Out of Nowhere' by Johnny Green and Edward Heyman. We will first play it with the familiar bass line:

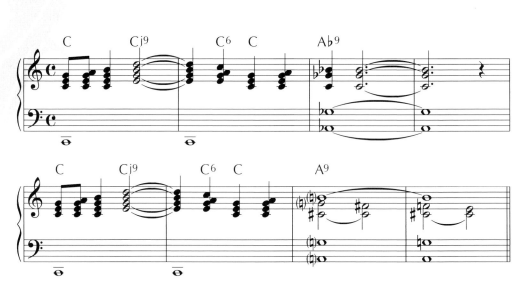

Out Of Nowhere (Edward Heyman/Johnny Green)
© 1931 by Famous Music Corporation.
© renewed 1958 by Famous Music Corporation

The full chord is played in the right hand, the bass note alone or the seventh interval is played in the left hand: this has been our way of harmonizing until now! We began working with this simple and accessible system and have become used to working in this way. As the bass has been separated from the chord we have been able to master the whole palette of chords that we had to learn. We have been able to understand the construction of each chord and have become familiar with playing the different chord shapes.

Now, we have to face the greatest opponent of our work – monotony. Monotony has occurred until now not only due to a lack of rhythmic movement – those long, sustained chords that hang on, rigid and motionless for a whole bar at a time. No, perhaps without noticing it consciously, the constant similarity of the way we arrange the chords has left us with a rather limited musical menu.

We have to face up to the fact that until now our only concern has been to get to know all the necessary chord components and chords and how to link these chords to form modules. Yes, we know them all now, all our X, X^6, X^7, X^9, X^+, $X^{7/+}$, $X^{7/6}$, X^{9-}, $X^°$, X^{j7}, X^{j9}, Xm, Xm^6, Xm^7 chords. And we are now quite familiar with playing these chords. We have also learned whole songs to observe the different

chords in context and to get used to playing longer chord sequences without having to look at printed music.

Now we have reached the stage where no chords are strangers to us. We can therefore gradually turn our attention to other tasks, certain practicalities to tackle the prevailing monotony of our playing. For this we need, above all, alternatives to the way we have been playing until now.

One of these alternatives is a different kind of bass. I do not mean a kind of bass that introduces rhythmic interest. We will come to that later in the chapter on rhythm. We will then move the bass around a bit more. The more quickly the bass moves, the more rhythmic the overall sound. Boogie-Woogie, with its breakneck bass movement, is the best example of this. But this is not our concern just at the moment. What I want to show you now is another kind of bass that does not improve the rhythm, but brings a new tone colour into play. Of course an alternative such as this can only be used here and there at suitable places as a contrast.

For this purpose we can omit the usual bass line and simply double the melody – one octave lower:

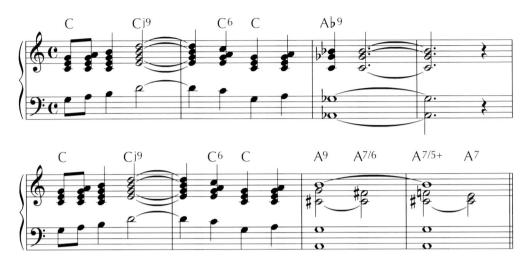

You can see that we have used this little trick only for two bars at a time before going back to the seventh interval in the bass. Somehow this is not yet quite right. The finishing touch is missing. We will add this to the bass melody by adding a series of ornamental notes a semitone below the melody notes, from which you slide up to the melody.

This will need a bit of practice until you achieve the right balance of sound. This additional activity in the left hand should not be at all bumpy. The flow of the melody should not be interrupted by this little acrobatic motive. You can also, as previously mentioned, only use this in certain places; usually at those places where the melody remains within the range of a few notes and does not make any wide leaps. It is a spice that can only be used occasionally and then in small doses. But it can relax our playing a little here and there.

It is not necessary to play these grace notes with each note of the doubled melodic passage. It is quite enough if you occasionally add one on the most important notes as, for example, in this transition of a song that you will most probably know:

Strangers in the Night (Bert Kaempfert/Charles Singleton/
Eddie Snyder)
© 1966 by Champion Music Corporation
and Roosevelt Music Co.,Inc., New York, N. Y.

There are many ways in which we can make our playing more varied and less monotonous. The choice of songs and the order in which you will later play them is a very important matter. A pianist in a cocktail-bar quite consciously changes from a lyrical to a rhythmic melody. He or she would also not play too many songs in major keys before adding a piece in a minor key. The minor mode creates a completely different background of sound, a completely different, melancholy sound. In this respect you could say that minor chords belong to the group of exotic chords.

Which minor key goes well with C major? According to the key signature, A minor should, as it has the same key signature – that is, no accidentals! So in C major the G^7 chord almost always leads towards C chords, but sometimes in exceptional cases, it manoeuvres the melody into A minor.

It is therefore quite appropriate in this chapter that we should now intensively study musical passages and whole songs in minor keys for the first time.

This should not lead to the misconception that G^7 is the seventh chord that usually leads to A minor. No, the dominant seventh or ninth chord is E^7 or E^9. The fundamental and typical A-minor pattern is: Am - Dm - Am - E^9. Many Gipsy songs and other pieces in the minor key are based on this structure.

Just for fun, we could let in an exotic chord, F^9, which sounds very good. In principle it has to be said that minor textures have much more colour and expressiveness than melodies in major keys.

As minor melodies have more colour anyway, they hardly ever use the Merry-Go-Round of Fifths. They simply do not need it. In certain circumstances the B^7 chord might occasionally be added before E^7, but that is all.

148

Here is another typical example from Gipsy music:

The B[7] could be substituted by the exotic F[7] chord, and the Gipsies do this frequently. To be precise, this should not be regarded as a substitute, as the exotic F[7] without doubt sounds much more interesting and complementary than the B[7] whose place it takes.

In the examples of minor melodies given so far, the connection with C major has not been obvious. For this reason we shall now take a look at 'Olga's Lullaby'. It is a very slow waltz with beautiful harmonies.

It has a beautiful melody and a beautiful chord progression! In the sixth bar there is a chord symbol that we have not yet examined. In spite of this, you should not have a problem understanding it. $B^{7/5-}$ can only mean that in this B^7 chord, the fifth step is lowered by a semitone.

The last chord in the eighth bar, G⁷, indicates that the melody will change over to C major. We will now follow the course of this song, as in 'Olga's Lullaby' we find the whole complement of beautiful chords that can appear in a standard in the minor mode.

This song also has 32 bars, but does not keep to the usual scheme. Bars 17–24 cannot be regarded as a bridge as they do not contrast particularly with the development of the melody, but fit in nicely with the main theme. The composer has not concerned himself with a particular pattern or rules. He lets his melody simply unfold in the way that sounds most natural.

Now let us go to the piano. Deal with the chords of each individual bar, hold each one, without going any further and listen to the sound of each. Most of the chords are familiar to you. This time we have not kept so strictly to our bass scheme. For example, there is an E⁷ chord in which the key note *e* and the third, *g sharp*, are played close together as a result of the overall spacing.

You can learn a lot from this song and I advise you to learn it well. All the chords that can possibly appear in a song in A minor are present here. Even the change to the relative major, C, is carried out fully and in detail. Following this, opening with an E⁷ chord, is a particularly exquisite passage in which the chord sequence leads back to the key of A minor. The key figure here is the exotic F⁷ chord.

As the song is written in a slow 3/4 time, the chord progressions are clear to see. You might have noticed that there are hardly ever heralds before seventh chords in minor keys. There are so many lovely chords to choose from that one is not dependant on playing heralds.

I would like to show you, briefly, the most important chords in the key of A minor by means of an A minor scale.

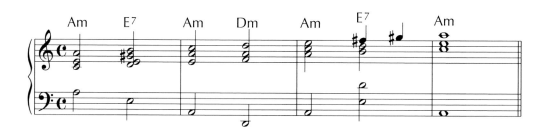

The chords are all complete here, except for the last E⁷ where we could not add the *e* in the right hand. You can see that *d, e* and *f sharp* would have been too close together. I know that it could be rather confusing to see a chord sometimes in its complete form and other times with one of its notes missing. But I'm sure that you now realize that this is usually done when there is no space, or also if the note in question already appears in the bass and would only be doubling this. So it is quite all right to play the E⁷ in the first bar

152

without the *e* in the right hand. You can choose whichever you prefer by playing the chord both ways: an unnecessarily full sound or a lighter chord. You know that there are three different minor scales. In this example we have chosen the melodic minor scale. The uphill route differs from the downhill – the descent must therefore be harmonized differently.

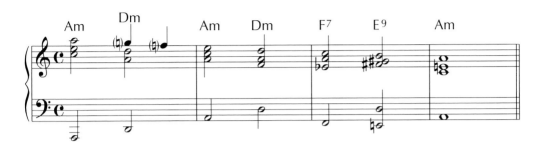

The D minor chord is based on the fourth step of the A minor scale. It is a very important chord in the progression of sounds. F is also a very important chord, in C – a key in which we are very much at home – occurring on the fourth step of the scale. The chords of both F major and F minor appear in songs in C major as supporting elements of the chordal texture. There are a great many folk melodies that use only three basic chords for their accompaniment.

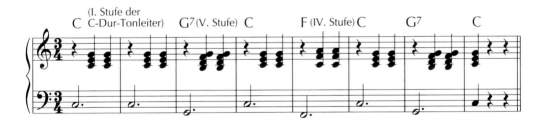

But this is only by the way! I think we have heard enough about A minor to deal with most songs that are written in this key.

There is another minor key more closely related to C major that we should now examine: C minor. In the first chapter we learned that the minor triad differs from the major triad only in that the third step is a semitone lower.

To be able to deal well with all songs that are written in C minor, it is necessary to take a close look at the three C minor chords – Cm, Cm^6 and Cm^7 – as well as the three minor chords of the fourth step – Fm, Fm^6 and Fm^7, as the first chapter, in which these were dealt with, is a long way back.

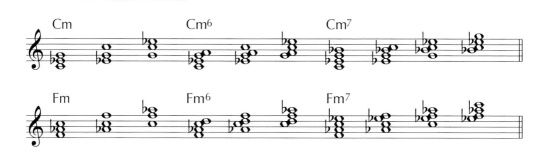

Cm^7 and Fm^7 look the most complicated, particularly in their inversions. But take comfort in the fact that these two very rarely occur in the standard repertoire.

The key of C minor is much closer than A minor, although C minor has a key signature with three flats at the beginning of the stave. This is because the key of C minor uses the same seventh chords as

C major (G^7, G^9, $C^{7/+}$, $G^{7/6}$, G^{9-}). These are well known to us. As already stated, F minor occurs the most often, as well as D^7. The exotic chords F^7, $B\flat^7$, $E\flat$ and $A\flat$ also make occasional appearances in the regions of C minor.

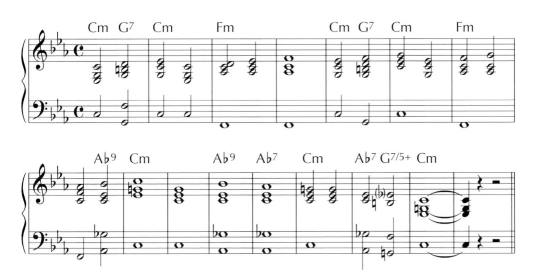

The exotic chord $A\flat^9$ appears here four times. It has the same relationship to C minor (in terms of steps) as F^9 has to A minor. According to the key signature its relative major would be $E\flat$. In this connection, I would just like to remind you briefly of the $E\flat^9$ chord from page 136, I mean the second chord of the system, which we referred to as the filler section C - $E\flat^9$ - Dm^7 - $D\flat^{11+}$ - C^9. This $E\flat^9$ was added in the key of C major as an exotic chord. Here, with a melody in C minor, it is not at all exotic. It is the relative major chord of C minor and is thus closely related. As the minor mode is rather romantic anyway, an $E\flat^7$ is quite enough to maintain the melancholy mood. You do not need any ninth chords for this.

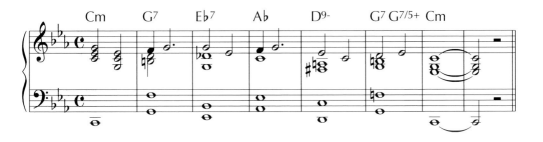

Standards and pop songs in minor keys are relatively rare. But strangely enough, many composers had unexpected – even sensational – success when they did actually create a song in the minor.

The song 'Summertime' from the opera *'Porgy and Bess'* (the first American opera!) by George Gershwin became the outstanding song of this opera over-night and was a success all over the world. It was similar for the Beatles thirty years later with 'Michelle'. Also, the Frenchman Francis Lai did not imagine when he wrote the music for the film 'Love Story' that his minor melody would become such a world-wide success.

This shows that minor keys create a strongly sentimental, romantic and exotic effect. They belong to the world of exotic sounds, without doubt. And these exotic sounds always enrich the more usual palette of sounds.

CHAPTER 7

MORE COLOUR THROUGH CHROMATICISM

If we take a retrospective look at the progress made so far, we can see that we have already passed through many important stages. Each of these stages has brought us significantly closer to our ultimate aim of being able to play the piano freely and without printed music.

We have learned that chords are constructed from the notes of scales. We have got to know the basic elements, the components of the different types of chords, and have dealt with their inver-sions and other variants. We then began to add one chord to another and gradually acquired the ability to think and work in modules. And soon we recognized that these modules link together to form module chains. We then tried to build these modules and module chains into sections of melodies, learned to harmonize whole pieces with them, and endeavou-red to move our perceptive faculty as far as possible away from the visual image of the printed music and towards acoustic sensitivity to sounds. We then completed the series of chords by adding and explo-ring the missing exotic varieties. In all these laudable endeavours we were fully absorbed in taking in and dealing with the essentials and could not spend any time playing around. In our work with different chord chains, one chord was always added on to the next and so on. There were of course quite a few semitone steps in the course of the different melodies. We then simply took a suitable chord from some-where to harmonize these notes that dance out of line.

159

Strangely, though, we never considered that we might not have to roam so far to find a chord for such an out-of-line semitone. Theoretically, there is nothing to stop us from simply pushing the previous chord up or down a semitone.

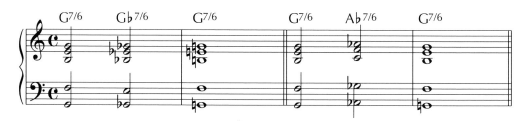

Anyone who plays the guitar will know this trick of adding colour to the sound. With barré fingering on the guitar you can move the same chord up and down, whereas on the piano you have to think about the new hand position.

It is also easy to do this on the Hawaiian guitar, as a metal bar is laid across the strings and moved up and down so that any chord can be moved up or down a semitone or several tones, in the most simple way. It is this semitone movement, upwards and downwards, that gives Hawaiian music its typical character.

In almost all Hawaiian melodies you hear this upward and downward movement of chords, and it is not difficult to imagine how the metal bar is moved up and down the strings, sometimes straight across the slim body of the Hawaiian guitar, sometimes at an angle, depending on the type of chord being played.

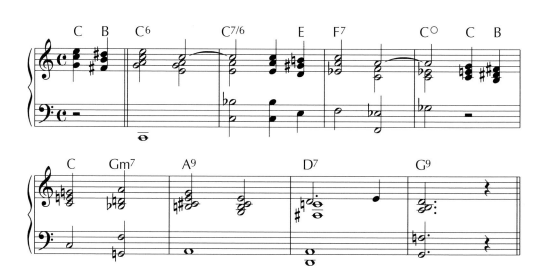

This type of chromatic chord, such as that produced by the simple metal bar, is not particularly suitable for our piano playing. So I will not ask you to work with this. On the piano we have quite different and much more effective ways of using the chromatic.

In contrast, listen to this chromatic transition that is frequently used in jazz compositions and sophisticated standards. It is a chromatically descending ninth chord (a ninth chord descending in semitone steps) whose journey could theoretically go on for ever. It is very easy to play if you take it slowly, but it sounds very complicated and creates amazing colour in the sound. The left hand has only two notes to move, the right hand has three.

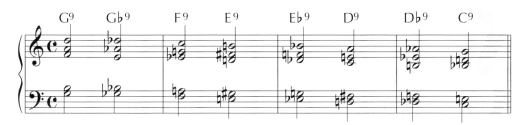

Usually only three or four of these chords are played in a row. Chord combinations such as these can be played in any key.

Here we are not working to the principle that different kinds of chords, determined by the melody, are linked together as has usually been the case in our examples until now. No, here the same chord – usually a ninth – is moved down in semitones. As I have already mentioned, such chromaticism cannot be continued for more than three or four syllables of the text. If you continued for longer than this, as sometimes happens in jazz or film music, where it is used to create a certain effect, it could upset the natural course of the melody. The chromaticism would not lead to the right harmonies and the connection with the theme of the song would be lost.

Oddly enough, the chromatic downwards spiral of ninth chords does not easily reverse direction, at least not in songs. In film music, however, great effects can be achieved with such a chord in ascending motion, for example to create the sound of a train approaching, if the tempo is increased at the same time. Or film music might use an ascending chromatic to express an emotional dramatic event: fear, horror or an impending catastrophe.

In songs and standards the spiral descends. The passage thus acquires a melancholy, plaintive character. This is also the reason why this practice is often encountered in blues, which usually conveys a plaintive message.

The most famous example of chords descending by semitone steps is probably Duke Ellington's 'Sophisticated Lady'. The text, by Mitchel Parish and Irving Mills, tells the story of a once delightful and shy young girl who, after years in the company of high society, becomes increasingly superficial and snobbish.

I will now show you a few bars of this melody by Duke Ellington, which I have transposed from A flat major to F major as the key of A flat major is rather too far from our usual field of action. We have not yet played in the key of F major, but you will see that it will not be difficult. You must simply observe that there is one flat in the key signature. Besides, there is only one single F major chord in this section and we have often come across this chord in our musical examples.

It must be pointed out that the chromatic transitions are extremely difficult. The first is particularly unusual. Here Ellington uses descending seventh intervals in the left hand and in the right hand he takes the full basic chord: $E\flat^7$ - D^7 - $D\flat^7$ - C^7. The chords are all quite easy to understand and actually do not conceal any mysteries. But moving from one chord to the next is not easy.

In the same short passage there is a second chromatic descent over four steps. This time Ellington uses the transition in ninth chords that we already know from the previous example, in which the left hand plays thirds. He takes the four stages: F^9 - E^9 - $E\flat^9$ - D^9. The third in the bass is actually written as a tenth in Duke Ellington's original version, which we wanted to avoid as not everyone's hands are big enough to stretch a tenth. There is no difference in the notes as the third (e.g. *f* - *a*) consists of the same notes as the tenth (*f* - *a*).

There is a certain difference in the sound. The tenth in the bass sounds fuller in tone as it brings in a broader spectrum of sound. Now let us look at the short section of the Duke Ellington melody 'Sophisticated Lady'.

Sophisticated Lady (Duke Ellington/Mitchell Parish/Irving Mills)
© 1933 by Mills Music, Inc.

Can you manage that? You must remember that you are now tackling the most difficult manoeuvres that appear in standards. Here you can really no longer talk about primitive pop songs. These are sounds that are otherwise only found in pieces by Debussy, Ravel or other similarly impressionistic 'classical' composers. Of course there are other quite different and much more complicated effects. This cannot be denied. But we are now no longer simply reading the notes. We are trying to play by ear, which forces us to create the harmonies of a particular song by ourselves. This is quite a big step forward and a great achievement. This cannot be done in the twinkling of an eye, of course. We take our task in hand, work slowly through the various stages and do not shy away from difficult assignments. Besides, we have enough time to digest such chord passages by means of many other examples.

Personally, I would advise you not to use the kind of harmonization shown in the first example when you encounter a descending chromatic passage in a song. Learn the descent with ninth chords and thirds in the left hand. This is a form that you can easily get to know and that is easy to use where appropriate.

This kind of harmonization is used not only in melodic passages. It can also be used as a filler. Although it would be unusual to use full chords as used in the previous example. It would look something like this:

The first chord (Gm^7) does not belong to the descending ninth sequence. It is just a connecting chord between the last chord of a section of a song to be followed by a filler (probably a C^6, a G$^{7/6}$ or similar), and the three chromatic steps. As the last step is a G^9, there is a good connection for the continuation of the C major song in question.

Within the normal course of a song there are naturally relatively few places where the melody descends by two, three or four semitone steps. Of all the existing standards there are hardly a dozen.

A melody that I have in mind just now is the song 'You Brought a New Kind of Love to Me' from the film *'The Big Pond'*, in which Liza Minelli plays the leading role and which tells the story of an unsuccessful tenor saxophone player. The music and words were written by Sammy Fain, Irving Kahal and Pierre Norman. We have transposed the passage to F major again so that it begins in a familiar key.

You brought a New Kind of Love to Me (Sammy Fain/Irving Kahal/Pierre Norman)
© 1930 by Famous Music Corporation, New York, N. Y.
© renewed 1957 by Famous Music Corporation

Here we find the same ninth-chord sequence that we have encountered before.

It seems as though it is often the composers of film music who use the chromatically descending ninth chords in their songs. In the theme song of the classic film *'Picnic'* with William Holden and Kim Novak – the title of the song is 'Moonglow' – there is also a melodic section with a chromatic descent which is harmonized with ninth chords descending in exactly the same order. Only this song is written in G major. So the chord steps begin a whole tone higher than in our last example.

G⁹   F#⁹   F⁹   E⁹

Moonglow (Will Hudson/Eddie de Lange/Irving Mills)
© 1934 by Mills Music, Inc.

The music and words of 'Moonglow' were written by Will Hudson, Eddie de Lange and Irving Mills, who we already know as one of Duke Ellington's lyricists. Mills, by the way, did not only write texts for Duke Ellington, he was also his manager, recording director and publisher.

I think we have now come across enough examples that use sequences of ninth chords descending in semitone steps. But such chromaticism is used as a means of expression and tone colour not only with full chords. You can also move parts of a chord chromatically and indeed downwards or upwards! If you move parts of a chord you bring not only colour, but

also rhythm into play, as one and the same chord produces more notes and so relieves the monotony of long sustained chords.

If part of a chord moves like this and changes, you might of course consider that it is no longer the same chord, but that by shifting one part of the chord three different chords are produced. In this example the chords were C - Dm⁷ - D#° (or E♭°) - C. In principle this makes no difference as if you did not move parts of the chord, it would just stand still. You can therefore regard this movement as a pure transition. Here are examples of the same steps in different positions:

We should not be concerned that everything sounds rather thin and primitive here. For the time being we are simply dealing with the principle of chromatic movement of parts of a chord. This can be done in a much more compact way and with quite different rhythms, and the bass does not have to move simultaneously in semitone steps. So we find, for example in 'Moonglow', the following two bars, in which the lower parts of the right-hand chord move up and down chromatically. This example has a 'bounce' rhythm; there is a certain rhythmic shift of the strong beats of the bar:

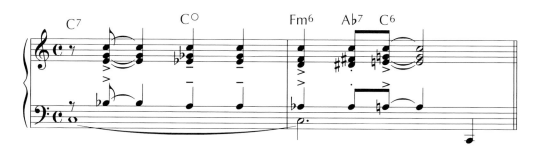

Sometimes the bass may rise chromatically to a relatively high pitch, which means that the chords of the right hand have to be arranged accordingly. This often happens when a song begins with a chromatically rising phrase.

The melody tinkles upwards in semitones while the bass takes first a whole tone step, and then two semitone steps. In the following bars there are more chromatic passages, the last of which serves as a filler.

The example is taken from an old standard. You do not need to learn this or think any further about it. The harmony is rather contrived and does not bring us any closer to our aim of being able to harmonize melodies ourselves. Here each note has been carefully considered before being written down. We need to be able to place our chords from our minds, directly on to the piano and have certain chord progressions and modules ready to place immediately and appropriately to accompany a beautiful melody.

So, if we wish to use chromaticism to increase the diversity of our playing, we need to have particular modules at hand. You have already encountered one, which is very useful, and that is the downwards spiral of ninths with thirds in the bass, which is quite easy to learn. Please learn it off by heart. Divide it into three sections as you can only use a short progression at a time.

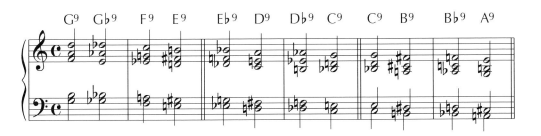

These units can be made use of in various ways. For example, when the melody descends chromatically. They can also be used in moving from one chord to another of distant relationship, which cannot easily be reached in a more direct way. They also function as a transition from one song to another in a different key. In some places you can also use them as fillers. Chromatic passages are however particularly suitable for introductions or preludes to a song. These passages not only bring an alternative touch to the overall sound, but they can also be very helpful.

I will now show you a second type of chromatic movement, with which you should become familiar as it can be useful in many situations. It can be put into practice both ascending and descending. Here only the bass and melody are moving by step, while in the right hand we play chords that we have known for a long time.

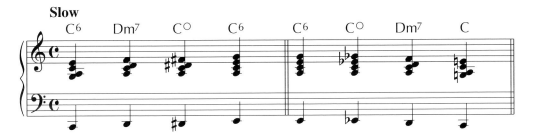

Please do not let it worry you that the symbol for the fourth chord is C^6 although there is an **e** in the bass. The bass note does not always have to be **c** in a C chord. You can use one of the alternative notes **e** or **g**, which we will discuss later. The third chord symbol is C°. This chord could have been called D#°, F#° or A°. With diminished chords you can use practically

any component as the key note, although it is perhaps more appropriate to keep to the rule of naming it according to its bass note.

You can of course force the rhythm in these rising and falling passages by replacing the crotchets with a dotted quaver followed by a semiquaver.

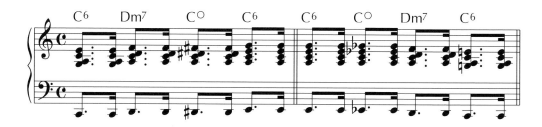

This use of chords and rhythm is typical of the blues. In blues you often find triplets

instead of dotted rhythms, or sometimes even both.

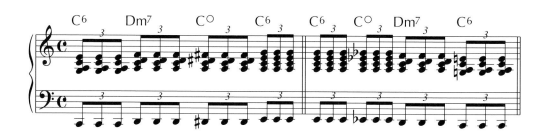

It is best to look straight away at one of the most well-known and most frequently-played blues: 'Basin Street Blues' by Spencer Williams. We will play not only the refrain but also the verse. Let

us begin with the verse and, first of all, just the few opening bars. As there is no melody in the second bar, just four beats' rest, we need a filler. Spencer Williams, the composer, did not grow any grey hairs over this. He simply repeated the first bar one octave higher and this solved the problem for him.

168

If a whole bar is available as a filler, it is not a bad idea to simply repeat the previous bar one octave higher. With blues it is possible to make a mistake: by playing too fast. The slower you play it the better. Imagine how you would approach a blues song if you were playing the trombone. The trombone has a soft, melancholy sound with very expressive qualities and is thus an instrument ideally suited to the blues, which always has a story to tell. This is why famous trombonists such as, for example, Jack Teagarden were most successful with blues melodies. Apart from this, the trombone comes closest to the sound of the human voice.

It is no coincidence that Spencer Williams fills the empty melody bar simply by repeating the musical idea of the first bar. Repetition is an essential element of blues. It is always carried out by a different instrument. Let us assume that the trombone plays the first section of the melody, then the trumpet repeats the same phrase an octave higher. Or a female or male singer sings the first phrase, which is then repeated by the trombone as a kind of echo. Blues is always a question and answer. There are many blues songs in which the phrases of the text are always sung a second time, that is repeated.

Blues is perhaps the most interesting form of jazz, as it is the oldest and has a completely original construction, which we will discuss later. Let us first look at the two bars, the second of which repeats the first.

We already know that blues is played very slowly, that repetition is introduced and that it has a distinctive, very accentuated rhythm. It is usually characterized by the use of dotted quavers or quaver triplets. It is syncopated at certain places, such as here in the last two chords of the bar.

Furthermore, there are certain preferred notes used in the melody. If we remain in C major, it is the following notes:

I do not wish to claim that in blues only these notes are used. But these are the most commonly used notes. Of these, the **b flat** and **e flat** stand out of course. The **b flat** is used simply as a passing note, as we saw in the last example.

You can see from the chord symbol that the **b flat** is intended to be a passing note as there is simply a C major symbol rather than C^7. In accordance with the feel of blues, there is no change of chord, the melody has just made a little detour to pass by its beloved flat.

It is a little different with the **e flat**, to which blues melodies are also closely attracted. In this case a chord is usually intended, that is the chord of F^7 or sometimes D^{9-}. But the **e flat** can also just as easily be used as a passing note.

Very slow

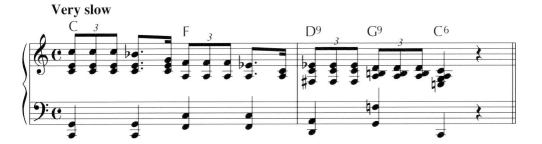

Earlier, you heard that with a low bass just one note is used if possible to avoid buzzing. Fifths, however, as often found in the bass of blues songs, actually sound very good. They have a rather elemental quality that is strongly reminiscent of Celtic music in which the bagpipes always play the drone. But let us get back to 'Basin Street Blues' and complete the verse of this song.

Basin Street Blues (Spencer Williams)
© 1928, 1929, 1933, 1987 Edwin H. Morris & Co.
A division of MPL Communications, Inc.

The trombones or trumpets of course usually freak out a bit in the last bar and instead of Spencer Williams's strict setting, play their hot favourite blues notes.

From here we go back to the beginning of the verse, which is on page 169 and play through the whole thing again.

171

In blues there are no gaps or monotonous rhythms: something happens on every crotchet beat. The tempo is slow, but it marches on and on. At the very moment when something might become monotonous, the instruments begin to play triplets. At this slow tempo musicians also like to pull the notes up and down a bit, in a similar way to the Hawaiian guitar. The trombone is particularly effective in using this technique as the slide can move backwards and forwards. This is why trombonists usually enjoy playing the blues.

Here is the whole refrain:

Basin Street Blues (Spencer Williams)

With 'Basin Street Blues', we have learned a complete blues with verse and refrain. We can see from the verse that the blues often uses chromatic progressions. Introductions and fillers also often use chromaticism. The same applies to endings, which in blues often look something like this:

Introductions also use chromatic chord progressions in this way, with sequences of triplets. There are of course many variations which, however, look very similar in terms of rhythm.

In the third bar we find the favourite notes *c - b flat - g - f - e flat*, which always make an appearance somewhere in the blues. They could have continued further in the last bar, which would have sounded more melancholy:

The D^{9-} in the second bar includes – rather unusually – an *f*, even though the thumb is playing an *f sharp*. You will be surprised to hear that this does not sound dissonant, but rather unusual. The favourite notes *b flat* and *e flat* in general lend a certain feeling of sadness and sorrow. This is also quite logical, as these two notes are main elements of the C minor scale. Blues texts tend, on the whole, to be very sad and lamenting: St. James's Infirmary – Jailhouse Blues – Down Hearted Blues – Bleeding Hearted Blues – Baby Have Pity On Me – Moan You Mourners – Grave Yard Dream Blues – Cemetery Blues – My Sweetie Went Away – Haunted House Blues – Wasted Life Blues – Sing Sing Prison Blues – Woman's Trouble Blues – Dying Gambler's Blues – Muddy Water – Send Me to the Electric Chair – Homeless Blues – Looking for My Man Blues – Sorrowful Blues – Lou'siana Low Down Blues – Work House Blues – Weeping Willow Blues – Empty Bed Blues – Poor Man's Blues – He's Gone Blues – Lonesome Desert Blues – Lost Your Head Blues – Hard Time Blues, and so forth, and so on.

These are really dreary titles. And they really do all exist. Most of them were sung by the unforgettable Bessie Smith, who died very young in an accident. Another world-famous singer, Billie Holiday, sang a lot of similarly sad songs. So for practically every difficult situation in life there is an appropriate blues title.

In a few exceptional cases, blues can be friendly, even happy, such as in our 'Basin Street Blues', where the narrator is looking forward to returning to New Orleans.

174

There are also a few very quick pieces that are wrongly called blues, such as 'Bye-Bye Blues', for example, seen on page 138, which you can now play from memory. 'Limehouse Blues' by Philipp Braham, inspite of the word blues in the title, is also very lively and in terms of tempos has nothing in common with the casual, lazy, almost shuffling character of the real blues. If you look at the words, however, which Douglas Furber wrote about the 'boy of Limehouse' – 'Poor broken blossom and nobody's child' – then it really is a blues. You can only imagine that Furber wrote the text of a blues song and that Philipp Braham wrote a fast song without worrying about the text.

Nowadays the blues is played not only in New Orleans, but throughout the whole world. Many blues singers, and practically all blues musicians are able to sing or play not just particular blues songs, but simply to play the 'blues'. That means they keep to an exact blues scheme that enables them to play freely around it. So they improvise, and compose their own quite private impromptu blues with the help of this scheme. And the blues singers sing along – about whatever is troubling them at the time.

Blues texts are usually short phrases, which may be repeated as a kind of answer by an instrument – such as the trombone or trumpet. This gives the singer time to think up the next section of text. If the singer is really troubled and suffering, the words of the lament flow as if straight from the heart. The instruments join in and a new blues song is born. The blues is the most peaceful, comforting and human way to rid the soul of bottled-up troubles and sorrow.

We require, as already mentioned, a fixed blues scheme. This fixed scheme is 12 bars long and no more. These 12 bars can of course be repeated as many times as you and the other players wish. If we count the number of bars in the refrain of 'Basin Street Blues', we must unfortunately observe that it is 16 bars long. It is thus not an authentic blues song as it does not keep to the blues scheme.

As we now know that the real improvised blues has 12 bars, it would be interesting to discover the scheme on which the chord progression is based. It makes sense that there must be a quite definite sequence of chords, otherwise the various instruments would not always be able to play the same chords with the certainty of sleep-walkers. The blues chord sequence looks like this:

175

According to this, we play three bars of C major chords, then one of C^7. These are followed by two bars of F^7, then two of C major again. In the last third of the sequence, there is one bar of G^7, one of F^7 and two bars of C major.

This is all very well, but what do we actually do with these chords? I mean, what rhythm shall we give them? If we want to play the piano in a blues band, we do not need to worry about the melody. On the contrary, we should play as little melody as possible so that we do not disturb the instrument playing the melody.

We could play all the blues passages we know, for example those from page 165, in the very simple form given there, with dotted quavers, with triplets, or with a mixture of these rhythms.

So, those were the C major passages. For C^7 we need to add a **_b flat_** somewhere:

For G^7 and F^7 we use the same arrangement of the chord, only four or five notes lower:

Now you know all the necessary rhythms and chords to be able to accompany a blues with the blues chord progressions, using chromatic passages.

It is of course clear that such a blues accompaniment is not a piece for solo performance. If percussion, bass and piano form the basis of a dixieland band, it is in the sense of a rhythm section. There is often also a banjo in a dixieland band. The rhythm section does not only produce the beat and drive, but also hammers out the chord structures and progressions. The solo instrumentalists and singer can then build their inspiration on this solid basis by keeping to the same chord sequence.

It is quite different, however, if you are sitting alone – with some kind of problems – at the piano or keyboard and want to express your troubled soul with your own, original blues. What do we do then? What do we do with the right hand? In such a case, I would say that the right hand should play as few chords as possible, as this hand has to play a melody that we do not even know. So it is best if the right hand has nothing else to worry about. This means that the left hand is required to play the full chord; a practice that we have not yet encountered, but one that will be very useful to us on many occasions.

We will play just two chords per bar with the left hand to make it easier to get used to this kind of accompaniment.

That was the first third of the blues pattern: $C/C/C/C^7$. Counting does not really help with a rhythm like this. There is nothing for it but to do what jazz musicians do: you have to tap the beat with your foot – either with the toe or the heel. Put a mat under your foot if people live in a flat beneath you.

Now we have to think up a melody. For this we first need a theme, a story that we want to tell. We do not need to use complicated sentences. Blues is a kind of lament. So we will complain about something. What do most people complain about? I think, about the weather – that it is constantly raining. So we will call our blues 'Rainy Day Blues'.

179

The first line could go like this:

Rainy, rainy, rainy day.

I admit, you could not call this a great poetic achievement. But we are no Shakespeare, but simple blues singers. If you say these words 'Rainy, rainy, rainy day' aloud and listen to the intonation, you will soon find the melody. Take the direction of the intonation and exaggerate it a little. This produces the following notes:

Rain - y, rain - y, rain - y day.

With this we already have the first two bars. This is because the second bar will be a repetition, whether by an instrument (in this case the piano) or the singer, who would sing the same words again.

Even in the second sentence, a blues singer would not strive to be particularly creative with the words. You are not trying to devise a perfect verse, but to express a feeling. In this case the feeling of the miserable rain. So you might add:

Ev'ry day's a rainy day.

Ev' - ry day's a rain - y day.

As this sentence will also be repeated, we can regard the first four bars – i.e. the first third of our blues – as being complete. So with everything added, it will look like this:

As there are no other instruments accompanying us to take over the repetition, we repeat the phrases ourselves on the piano, and perhaps, preferably, an octave higher so that the repetition has a little originality.

In the second third of the blues we have two bars of F^7 chords and two bars of C chords:

As we are forced to make up our text practically as we are singing, we will not have time to construct sensational verses. We will take the next few best words that occur to us that rhyme with 'day'. For example:

Skies are dark and clouds are grey.
Rainy, rainy, rainy day.

This gives us our text for the next four bars, i.e. for the second third of our 'Rainy Day Blues'. We have to take care with the melody as we can only use F^7 chords in the first two bars. F^7 does not contain an **e**, but an **e flat**, so we have to change our melody to use an **e flat** instead of the **e**.

To create the third and last section of our blues, let us first take another look at the blues scheme for the last four bars:

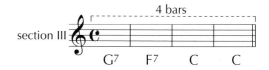

One bar of G^7, one bar of F^7 and two bars of C. The last two bars should somehow sound like an ending. For this, a passage using the preferred notes of a C major blues (**c - b flat - g - f - e flat**) would be suitable, perhaps also a few triplets. For the left hand, C minor would go better here than C major.

Of course we need to make our text fit with this passage. For the G^7 and F^7 sounds of the first two bars we need to think of something special. Another rhythm and a few words that sound a bit more sophisticated. How about this:

**Gets you down and dreary,
makes you sad and weary.**

We will sing most of the words of the first phrase on the note *g* and the second on the note *f*.

**Over hill, over plain,
Over meadow and lane,
The rain is coming your way.**

Okay we let the rain be our inspiration and so we were able to fabricate a complete blues song with text, melody and rhythm. In the last bar we briefly break away from C minor to give the sound more colour. We glide from A♭7 to G7. If you want to be particularly bluesy, you could utter one more exclamation, for example, 'Rainy Day!' or 'Oh yeah'. Here we glide again, this time from D♭9 to C9.

You could work in another typical blues feature, and this would go in bars 9 and 10 (C7 - F7). Blues specialists would play the **g** in the first bar and the **f** in the second as octaves and rock back and forth. The musical term for this is tremolo.

Our piece has become a genuine blues. The text expresses unhappiness: the unhappiness of weeks of continuous rain. A situation in which you can urgently make use of a blues song to sing away your soul's depressive mood.

Rainy, rainy, rainy day.
(Rainy, rainy, rainy day.)
Ev'ry day's a rainy day.
(Ev'ry day's a rainy day.)

Skies are dark and clouds are grey.
(Skies are dark and clouds are grey.)
Rainy, rainy, rainy day.
(Rainy, rainy, rainy day.)

Gets you down and dreary,
Makes you sad and weary.

Over hill, over plain,
Over meadow and lane,
The rain is coming your way.

We have made the melody as simple as it possibly could be. The phrases are short, following the rhythm of the words and with typical blues repetitions. The rhythm of the melody is emphasized by the sparing use of chords in the bass.

I will show you the whole thing again in one piece so that you can have a better general view.

Rainy Day Blues (Simon Schott)
© 1996 Schott Musik International, Mainz

185

In the last system you can see the importance of chromaticism, which is a frequently-used means of expression in blues. The way in which the main blues phrase moves in semitone steps at the end of most blues melodies, like the two chromatically descending final chords $D\flat^9$ and C^9, provides elements of musical colour and contrast such as can only be offered by chromaticism. So we should in future use this wherever there is a natural opportunity to do so.

1. Where the melody moves chromatically:

2. Where a chromatic bass line is used along with the resulting chromaticism in other parts of the chord:

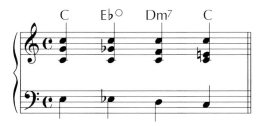

CHAPTER 8

RHYTHM – THE PULSE OF LIFE

Rhythm is the unseen creator of many works of nature and of human beings. So the surges of the sea, through the rhythm of the tides over millions of years, have created the most strange rock formations; the sculptor's statues gained their form through the rhythm of chisel strokes; the poet creates a drama through the rhythm of verses; our technical products are born through the rhythm of machines; so rhythm breathes life into all kinds of music.

The amazing creative potential of rhythm is to be seen clearly in classical music in particular: be it the precise, mathematical clockwork flow of a Bach fugue, the powerful throbbing of a Beethoven symphony or the delightful rippling evenness of a Schubert song. Without rhythm all this music would not exist.

And of course neither would so-called easy, popular music. Countless forms are created for the purpose of dance, which requires particularly pronounced accentuation to encourage the dancers to make certain movements.

Whether we are dealing with standards in the form of a foxtrot, one-step, charleston, tango, slow waltz, waltz or jazz waltz; with South American or Spanish rhythms; with jazz, boogie, rock and roll; with the many, many current types of rock or hard rock music, psychedelic, rap, disco, salsa, Latin American styles, reggae, heavy metal; the countless kinds of harmonically complex funk (black funk, British funk, American funk, soul funk, jazz funk, rock funk, disco funk, hard rock funk); or with acid, house music, hip hop, etc.; all these kinds of music are distinguished by their different rhythms.

You may be wondering why I chose to deal with the blues in such depth in the previous chapter; why I took such trouble to describe its construction. The reason is, because blues forms the basic

189

foundation of jazz and, in particular, the rhythmic examples for everything that remains for us to learn.

There are many people who believe that rhythm is something you either have or do not have. But this is wrong. There are certain techniques that produce rhythm in free piano playing. These techniques can be learned by anybody.

As you will have already noticed in the pieces that we have learned from memory, there are great differences in the independent rhythms of a melody. There are songs whose melodies contain all kinds of different rhythms. Other songs have rather static and boring melodies. It is with such songs, in particular, that you must find ways of bringing in some movement. If you have to deal with such boring, unrhythmic songs, in which the melody has long sustained notes – sometimes even over two bars – then you have to use some tricks to keep the momentum going.

Let us now deal thoroughly with the 'filler' theme. We have already encountered a few possible ways of filling empty bars.

1. *Repeat the previous bar*

This method is most commonly found in blues, which has a particular tendency to use repetition. If you turn back to page 169, you can see such repetition in the first two bars of 'Basin Street Blues'. This can only work when the musical phrases of the song are short and the bar to be repeated is complete in itself. A basic requirement is that one whole bar has no melodic phrase, as was the case in the short blues phrases.

With phrases that carry on for two bars or more, such as this one, repetition is not possible.

Sometimes it also happens that a filler has two bars available. Then of course there would be enough space for a repetition.

This kind of repetition is particularly appropriate if you are accompanying a singer, and thus when a text is being sung. In this case a musical echo of the last words sounds really good. But as mentioned, you need two whole bars for this.

In principle, it must be said that there are relatively few cases where a boring sustained note can be livened up by repetition. But there are other ways in which to fill empty bars.

2. Fill the bar with changing chords

There are many possibilities here. Look at the preceding melodic phrase to establish which note it ends on. In C major it could be one of many notes.

And then we should know which chord symbol is indicated for this last, sustained note in order to be able to add on a chain of further chords. Let us take the first example, which would probably have the following chord symbols:

The last two bars do not need to have the symbols added of all the chords that contain the *g* of the melody. That would mean adding seven different chords on G, one after another, so that something happens on every crotchet beat.

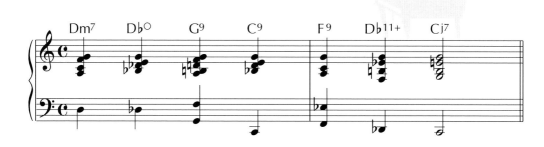

That is of course acrobatics. You have to play the most complicated chords in quick succession and even then you cannot say that such a filler sounds harmonically satisfying. Each sound is rather rushed.

Does a filler have to be so complicated? No, of course not! The reason why it was so difficult in this case is because we were tied to the melody note *g*. If we play the required *g* on the first beat only, but then go on freely to play other melody notes, the chords no longer present a problem. Then a whole host of harmonies are available for us to make use of.

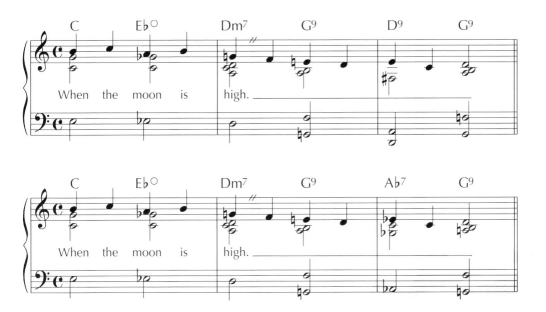

We did not need nearly as many chords for our filler. Only four instead of seven, as we held each chord for two melody notes. This of course requires us to be more inventive – to be a composer for a short passage. But this can only be a good thing as we must acquire this ability to improvise if we want to play the piano freely.

There is no need to 'reach for the stars'. We proceed as simply as possible, ascending or descending in steps or, at most, leaving a note out here and there.

We will now work through all six examples in this way. This will provide us with enough opportunities to practise this kind of little improvisation. Let us go on to example number two and try also here to find two different fillers. In this second

example, the melody ends on an *e*, which is ideally suited to a chord change. First of all think about the harmonies in this passage that could lead to the *e*.

So, this is a quite normal passage that occurs thousands of times in standards. There are many ways in which we could deal with this filler. We will select two of them. In the first and the second we will take a little ride on the Merry-Go-Round of Fifths, which would be appropriate here. We will simply take the melody as it comes in the first two bars.

Now here is the second example. As the **e** is so well suited to the Merry-Go-Round of Fifths journey, we will for once play a Merry-Go-Round chord on each beat in the first bar of the filler. But take a closer look at these four chords. You will see that they are very easy to play. I would like to urge you to learn the four chords of this first bar off by heart. Pay attention, in particular, to the bass, where fifths are played as the rest of the chord in the right hand is thinned, consisting now only of three notes.

In the third bar, the exotic chord $A\flat^7$ makes an appearance. This $A\flat^7$ can always be used in C major fillers. It fits in well whatever the position of the melody.

Let us now go on to case number three, in which the last note is the high **c**. With this melodic constellation, the chord progression will certainly lead to a C chord on the first note of the filler; either C^6 or C^{j7}. But, most probably C^6, which is more suitable as an ending note. So for example three, we could expect the following harmonization:

For the last eight-beat-long note **c**, the exotic $A\flat$ chord is again very suitable. We do not need any other chord. We simply let it run away from C^6 and run back to C^{j7}.

194

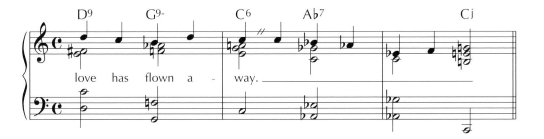

love has flown a - way. _____

For the second version of melodic example number 3, we will not exert ourselves, but simply use our old familiar module C - E♭° - Dm⁷.

love has flown a - way. _____

Both versions can be used for a final note in C major. But you must admit that the exotic A♭ chord is particularly suitable in this situation and sounds the most interesting.

Even if we are accompanying a singer, he or she will not hold this special end-note for the whole eight-beat duration. So we always have a certain amount of free space for our own selection of chord changes. I have written in a text for each practice example so that you can imagine how it might be if a singer was singing and you were to play after his or her last word to fill in the eight beats. Actually there are only seven, as the singer sings a word on the first beat of the first bar of the filler.

Now on to melody number four. This phrase also appears in thousands of standards. We can presume that phrase four is usually harmonized as follows:

The last note, on to which we must link our filler, is a **d** and the chord is G⁹. Here we are going to do something different. Please turn back to page 146. In the example shown there, we double the melody with the left hand in the bass. We

will now apply the same principle here to bring a bit of variety into our playing. And we will play three inversions of the Dm⁷ descending. The whole thing then looks like this:

I do not suppose that you will have any difficulty with the gliding downwards of the Dm⁷ chords: you can take it at a

suitably relaxed tempo. In the alternative example we can use our C - E♭° module again.

Fm^6 would also fit very well. You could use this in the same way as the Dm^7 in the example before last: with the melody doubled in the bass.

We should take this opportunity to remember that Dm^7 and F^6 are identical chords that differ only in their bass note and therefore can only be identified by looking at the bass note.

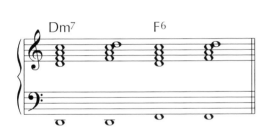

Fm^6 is similar, only it has a flat sign in front of the **a**, so the note becomes **a flat**. It is a lovely, colourful sound and is particularly suitable in such sequences of descending inversions for use in a filler.

Now we will deal with the fifth kind of melodic ending. Here we land on **b** and I can imagine that most of the many melodic phrases with this pattern use nothing other than the G^7 harmonization. It is a popular phrase, often used at the end of an introduction and as a lead into a refrain.

Here, again, we experience the phenomenon whereby the simplest kinds of melodic phrases present the greatest problems in fillers. It is really very difficult to add chords to a filler like this. Strange, diminished or exotic chords do not help us at all here. They sound completely out of place. So there is nothing for it but to resort to old fashioned chords and not too many at a time. Preferably with just one, or two at the most.

There is only one way in which we can prevent this becoming boring: when there are few chords – use a lot of melody notes. We must let the melody rise and fall so that there is plenty of movement.

In the second version of melody number five, we will use two chords. We will place the Dm^7 herald in front of the G^7 chord so that the character of this simple song phrase is not disturbed. A herald always has a close relationship with the target chord. It is experienced as a kind of suspension in the direction of resolution, almost as though the target chord is in two parts.

Melodic passage number six also ends on a G^7 chord (or perhaps on Dm^7) and, because of the f in the melody, presents us with similar difficulties to number five.

In the first version, which we end with a G^7 chord, and which represents the more popular treatment of a song, we add the herald Dm^7 once again. We also double the melody in the bass. In popular music there is really no alternative to this. You must use the herald whether you like it or not.

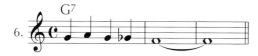

198

In the second version we will assume that we are dealing with a more sophisticated song. In such a case it is better that we do not stay on the Dm^7 chord, but make use of the rather exquisite sound of the D♭° chord, which goes rather well. Diminished chords provide a good alternative in many fillers.

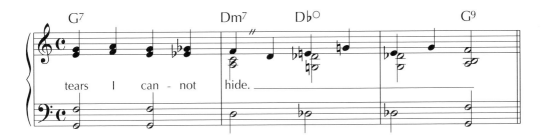

As we are assuming this to be a more sophisticated song, we will use G^9 as the final chord rather than G^7.

I hope that these six examples provide some inspiration and take us a bit further. So we have until now handled long, sustained final notes of melodic phrases in two ways: 1. By simply repeating the previous bar, and 2. by filling in the space with changing chords. With the second way, in more popular choral textures, we were forced to fill the bars with fewer chords and more melodic movement. There are, however, other possibilities of bringing life to empty bars.

3. *Fill by playing the chords*
   in two instalments

Compare our old familiar passage C - E♭° - Dm^7 - C played one chord per beat, with the method of playing just half of the chord on one beat and the other half on the next. With the same module you can then fill a much longer passage.

That was one chord per beat. There is no time for each chord to unfold, to make an impression, to create a mood. Now let us listen to the chords in their halved form. This version sounds a bit like the blues.

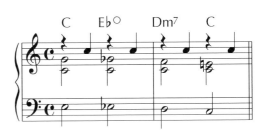

plicated a chord, the more possibilities there are. Let us take, for example, the G⁹ chord in its most commonly-used position:

What we are doing here is not new. If you look back at page 173, you will find the same passage with triplets, which often appears as the final module of a blues piece.

You can divide a chord in different ways. You can first play the upper part, the middle part, or the lower part, or two of these, then play the rest. The more com-

This is the easiest way to play it and has the fullest sound. The right hand does not even play all the notes of the chord. The *f* is not used in the right hand as it is already played by the left hand. Now which part of the chord shall we take first: the upper, the lower, or the middle part? Or shall we take the lower and middle parts together and the other two upper notes later?

We can of course give the second part of the chord all kinds of different rhythms.

With this kind of division of a chord it can happen, for example, that the seventh interval in the bass will suddenly be played

on its own. This does not sound very good. In fact it sounds rather inadequate. It is a good idea to add the third of the chord (the third step of the appropriate scale). Compare the sound of the two different bass patterns of a D^9, $D^{7/6}$, $D^{7/+}$, D^7 or D^{9-}:

left hand

If you like you can always add the third within the seventh interval. Now let us go on to our example of a rhythmic chord division. We have linked the chords D^9, Db^9 and C^9 in a rhythmic sequence:

You can easily construct examples such as this with any chord. I would advise you to do this above all with all the ninth chords that you have encountered so far. Apart from this we will come across such rhythmic fillers in the examples of standards given later.

4. *Filling by letting one note of the chord wander*

Theoretically you could let any note of a chord walk around a bit. In practice, however, particularly with complicated chords whose elements are already almost disturbingly close to each other, there is no room left. So we are in a position to make a passage more interesting by moving one note of a chord if there is a bit of space in the chord. You can often create a bit of space by forming the bass differently, for example: root and fifth – so the

fifth is not used in the right hand. In this way you save using that note in the right-hand chord, thus creating a gap.

But even then the note to walk around, in this case *f*, cannot wander very far. You can see that at the most it can descend by three semitone steps to arrive at *d*. It cannot go any further.

Usually you would move one or two semitones up or down, and no further. In context, this would sound something like this:

Here you might possibly query the fact that the third is included in the seventh interval with the chords A⁹, D⁹ and C⁹, but not with G⁹. Why are there always such confusing exceptions?

The sound is always our judge. Of course you could also add a third in the bass of the G⁹ chord. But this is just about the dividing line. If you descend any further,

two notes as close together as the key note and the third do not sound good at all. The fifth, however, still sounds pleasant. Please try this out with the E⁷ bass notes:

left hand

In general it has to be said that as far as these fillers with wandering notes are concerned, they too should only be used sparingly and should not appear in such an extended passage as shown in the previous A^9 - D^9 - G^9 - C^9 chord sequence.

5. *Filling by letting the bass march*

You will have heard this in brass band music, at the band stand, or as the band marches along the streets. The bass tuba plays two notes in succession as the basis of the popular chord – the key note and the fifth: the so-called alternating bass.

or in a waltz:

It might happen that you can use an alternating bass for standards and pop hits, but in general it is not appropriate. We have to find another way of moving the bass.

Perhaps you will remember our 'Bye-Bye Blues' from page 138. Of thirty two bars, twenty eight have only one chord in the bar. Each of these chords is thus held for four beats. Four bars are filled with minims. This might be quite all right when you have bass, drums and twenty other instruments to liven things up; but not when you are sitting alone at the piano. The way in which we have notated 'Bye-Bye Blues' on page 138 is a perfect

example of a melody without rhythm. Here something has to be done with the bass, preferably so that another bass note marches along on every crotchet beat. If you cannot think of a suitable left-hand line, you can always simply let the bass rise step by step in a scale passage. This should not present a problem. Of course with different chords we must use different scales. With a C major chord, the C major scale and with an A major chord, the A major scale, and so on. To bring a bit of variety to your playing you could always occasionally use a chord in two instalments. Or you could move one of the notes in the right hand instead of letting the bass wander. We can allow ourselves these little alternatives particularly in the passage with the module $C - Eb^° - Dm^7 - G^9 - G^{7/6}$ in the middle of the song. In all the other bars we will use the step-by-step ascending marching bass to provide the rhythm.

If you let this bass march more intensively, by using a dotted quaver rhythm instead of crotchets, and if you use a certain sequence of notes, you have a boogie-woogie pattern. There are thousands of bass, rhythmic, and melodic patterns from which you can create a boogie-woogie piece. We will take four bars of one of them.

left hand

And now we will add a short right-hand pattern. For example, the one we used on page 179 for the blues. Although there we played it with the left hand.

Boogie is a rhythmic form in which the bass marches along uninterrupted. You might have noticed that the harmonic progression consists of three bars of C^6 and C^7 in the fourth, just like the first four bars of a blues. This is no coincidence, as boogie is constructed on the blues pattern, as is rock'n roll. You will probably remember the blues pattern that we gave you for C major.

Nowadays not many people know how boogie-woogie was created. It was in the years of recession and unemployment, when out-of-work musicians formed bands in Chicago and other big cities in the USA, and drove through the city streets in old broken-down trucks. After playing one or two pieces they would stop and collect money from passers-by. For most of the instrumentalists the bumpy road surfaces and rocking movement of the truck was not a problem. Saxophonists, trumpeters, trombonists, were able to play their passages in a moving vehicle. The piano was placed on the loading area of the truck and the pianist had quite a problem playing the keys of the piano in a quick piece. In those days pianists played a so-called 'journey' in the left hand, which meant playing a deep bass octave with the thumb and little finger of the left hand, then leaping – often at a very fast tempo – to the middle of the piano, where they would hammer out the rest of the notes of the chord belonging to the bass. On solid, stationary ground this was no problem. But on a bumpy truck, many wrong notes were played. Some players then had the idea of keeping the hand still, placing it on the keys and moving only the fingers, without changing the hand position. This is how boogie-woogie was born.

If we want now to complete our boogie according to the blues model, we continue with the same pattern as that used for the first four bars, but keep to the given chord progression. The blues scheme of the second four bars looks like this:

For F⁷ we must of course take the F major scale as a basis and add a **b flat** to the bass melody.

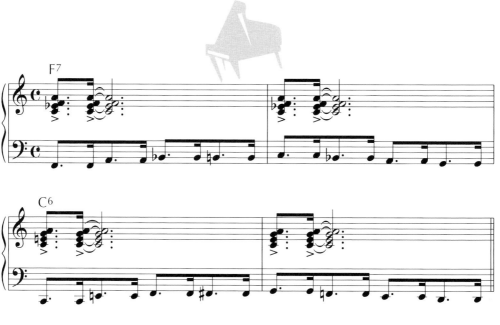

In the last third we are forced to depart from the bass pattern used so far as in the first two bars we change from G^7 to F^7, so we have only the space of one bar for each.

So here we have a complete, self-made boogie. As mentioned, there are many varieties of bass lines, some with only slight differences. So you could, for example, build octaves into the bass line shown.

Rock 'n roll is only slightly different from boogie-woogie in the bass. But the right hand on the piano, or the chord rhythms played by the band have a more strongly accented, stamping rhythm, which is often based on the following pattern of accented beats:

With this we will close our section of the 'filler'. We have learned five different ways of filling long, sustained chords:

1. *Repeat the previous bar*

2. *Fill the bar with changing chords*

3. *Fill by playing the chords in two instalments*

4. *Let one note of the chord wander*

5. *Let the bass march*

With these we have enough means at our disposal to liven up any sustained passage.

There are thankfully a great number of songs whose melodies already have a strong drive and so provide the desired rhythmic interest themselves. 'Sentimental Journey' by Bud Green, the band leader Les Brown and Les Homer, is one such standard.

To enhance this piece most pianists add the third above the melody and glide up to the target notes with short grace notes.

The best bass accompaniment to this is a boogie-woogie run, even if the song is not a boogie.

Of course we cannot use this pattern in all passages. Wherever it does not fit in, we have to build in something different. You can always learn the most by studying a whole song at once.

Sentimental Journey (Bud Green/Les Brown/Ben Homer)
© 1946 by Edwin H. Morris – Cappell & Co., Ltd. London
Cappell & Co., GmbH, München

This rhythmic standard should become a solid part of your repertoire. Divide it into four-bar sections and gradually learn them.

When a melody is filled with rhythm, you usually do not need such a busy left hand. It is often enough to let one chord ring on, preferably a beautiful, full, rather complicated chord.

In order to do this we must first get used to playing and changing complicated chords in the left hand. I will now show you a chord progression for the left hand. Each of these chords can be used later either individually or in combinations as shown here.

As we do not want to be fixed on C major songs for ever, the time has come to practise such chords in other keys. The best thing to do is to make a journey immediately to F major and G major, as in these keys we will encounter sounds that

are already familiar to us. Here, too, we are no longer trying to produce simple sounds, but to make use of the most interesting and colourful sounds. Again we play the whole chord in the left hand alone. For F major we need to learn the following combination:

You can hear that without an independent bass line the chords, which are almost without exception familiar to us, sound rather strange. But we must get used to this kind of harmonization. It is often urgently required, particularly when you want to

keep the right hand free from playing chords to handle rhythmic runs or rhythmically complex melodies. Perhaps we should take out the F^9, the $B\flat^6$ and the $B\flat m^6$ and introduce them once again individually as they may still be too unfamiliar.

To make things clearer, I have put the G^9 chord in its best position, before the F^9 in the same position, the C^6 chord is placed before the Bb^6 and the Cm^6 before the Bbm^6. You will recognize from this that the chord formations in other keys are iden-

tical to the ones we already know. We now want to move this series of left-hand chords without bass notes that runs from F^6 to C^9 up a whole tone, i.e. to transpose it to G major. There is therefore no flat in the key signature this time, but a sharp.

There is a very beautiful melody that goes very slowly yet is nevertheless extraordinarily rhythmic. Our chord progression in G major fits perfectly as a harmonization for this song. We will work through one

section of the song after another, four bars at a time. We will place the chord in the bass and play only the melody with the right hand.

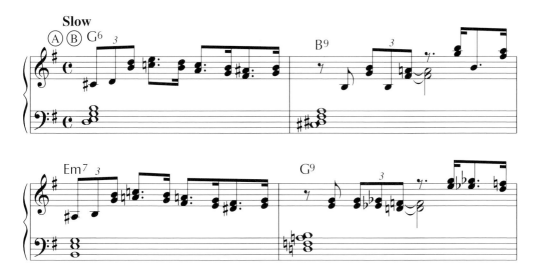

Twilight Time (Buck Ram/Morty Nevins/Al Nevins/Artie Dunn)
© 1944 by Campbell-Porgie Inc., 1619 Broadway, New York, N. Y.

As you can see, it is an exceedingly rhythmic melody. Here you need to tap your foot along to the very slow tempo, which should be around the metronome marking ♩c.56. With the right hand play only the melody, alone or in thirds, as you wish. If a little filler should be required, repeat a

few notes from the preceding section of the melody. Now let us look at the next section with C^6 - Cm^6 - G^6 and the Merry-Go-Round of Fifths E^9 - A^9 - Am^7 (herald) - D^9. The melody here is one of the loveliest ever harmonized by a Merry-Go-Round of Fifths.

Twilight Time (Buck Ram/Morty Nevins/Al Nevins/Artie Dunn)

If you had not played blues, boogie or jazz until now, you will need to overcome some difficulties with the rhythm of the melody. This anticipation of the beat practised with quavers, which is also known as 'bounce', looks rather confusing when written down. Personally, I do not like expressing such a rhythm for our own private use in complicated notation. If you can dance well and have a bit of rhythm in your body, it is not difficult to perform this bounce, adding slightly anticipated notes here and there in suitable places rather than keeping to an exact metronomic beat. With straight quavers you can easi-

ly notate the bounce rhythm without any confusion:

But when you are working with a triplet bounce rhythm, it becomes more complicated.

In our song we have notated the bounce rhythm as it is normally written. Now let us go on to the next system.

Next comes the middle section, also called the 'bridge'. We will look at the complete section, which consists of two parts that are almost the same, but at different pitches. As we have not come across B^9 very often, it is good that the first two bars are played entirely in thirds. Once you have learned these bars you will no longer be put off by a B^9 chord.

section A except for the last two bars, which are indicated with the bracket marked 2. From there we go on to the middle section, C, at the end of which is the indication Da Capo al Fine. Now you play the whole things from the beginning again and end with the bracket marked 3.

Now you have some hard work to do. Take your time and plough conscientiously through 'Twilight Time'. It is a standard well worth the trouble. Many pianists in international hotel-bars have chosen this as a theme song. That means it is played as the first and last song of each appearance.

That was probably the most difficult song we have played so far. I hope that you do not have any problems fitting the sections together. Keep in mind that section A is 8 bars long and that it goes back to the beginning at the first repeat sign. Then comes section B, which is identical to

It is quite possible that the bounce rhythm will give you a headache. So I would like to give you a few more examples in which the left hand takes over the chord progressions while the right hand plays rhythmic passages with bounce characteristics.

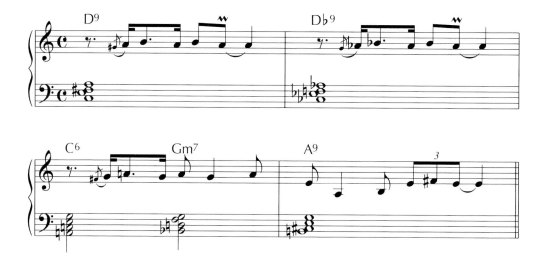

You should always learn such little improvisation models immediately. You can use them everywhere: in introductions, bridges, as postludes, etc. The difficulties in 'Twilight Time' were presented by the rather tricky right-hand bounce rhythm and the unfamiliar chord shapes, without an independent bass line in the left hand. I do not imagine that you found 'Twilight Time' particularly difficult although it was in G major rather than C major. Even if we explore F major in our next song, it should not present any problems as you will not come across a single unfamiliar chord in the whole piece.

We have after all worked through the whole litany of a broad sound spectrum in the sharp keys from C around to B^9 of the Merry-Go-Round of Fifths, and in the other direction, in the flat keys, from C around to Db^9. The construction of the chords is identical and we have examined each type of chord thoroughly so that the same chord type in another key appears like an old friend.

It must of course be accepted that, for example, a ninth chord in another key that lies four or five notes lower, cannot be played in exactly the same way. The whole thing has been pushed so far down that you can no longer play a third, a fifth or a seventh in the bass, but only a single, very deep note. We shall now address this problem systematically.

You will doubtlessly have noticed that we have gone on to play more and more full and complicated chords and are now using professional-sounding chords. If we look at the C major scheme, there are two groups of chords: the sevenths and the non-sevenths. The chords of the latter group are easy to identify and can be used immediately in all keys. For the normal C major chord we would usually play C^6 or in some, rarer, cases Cj^7. Both are easy to play in any key, whether you require F^6, G^6 or any other sixth chord. Minor sixth and minor seventh chords are just as easy to use. As there are only three diminished chords we do not need to worry about them.

That means we only need to concentrate on the seventh chords. As we hardly ever use the normal seventh chord, except with popular melodies, there remain three types: ninths, $^{7/6}$ and $^{7/+}$. The rare $^{9-}$ chord differs from the ninth only in that the ninth step is played a semitone lower.

So far the G^9 chord has been the most commonly used ninth chord. It can be used to harmonize melody notes within a whole octave, as can any ninth chords. In some cases both the two lowest notes, *a* and *b*, have to be played with the thumb.

In the bass you use the seventh interval *g* - *f* or, to create the fullest sound, the seventh interval with the third. Whether you play the additional third or not depends entirely on the instrument. On some pianos it creates a buzzing noise, on others it does not. Many keyboards take the third in the bass well, but not the electronic Fender.

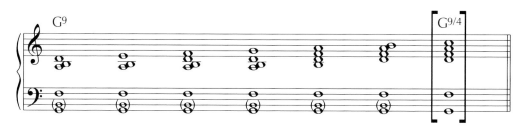

A ninth chord that we need quite often and that lies at a similar pitch is A^9.

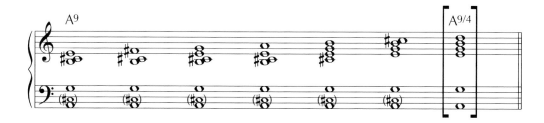

Because of the pitch, the D^9 close to the C^9 is played differently to the C^9. Let us just take a quick look at these chords.

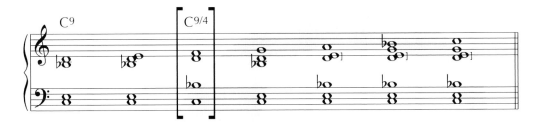

We have not added a bracket round the third of the C^9 chord as the bass is high enough here, so it would sound fine on most instruments. In the third chord we had to leave it out because, as you know, in a chord with the symbol 'sus 4' the fourth step is required instead of the third (see page 47).

To finish with, let us look at the positions of the D^9 chord, which are exactly the same, but one tone higher. This overview of the four most commonly found series of ninths should suffice for the time being.

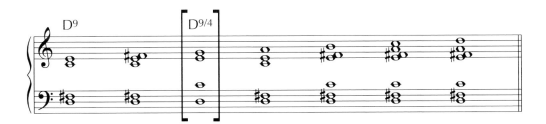

In the following song in F major you will now encounter some of these G^9, A^9, C^9 and D^9 chords in their various positions. It is a slow bounce rhythm: metronome marking ♩c.88. The chords that we will play are more complicated than those in their original form. Our sound is something like that often used in a jazz big-band arrangement.

Love is Just Around the Corner (Leo Robin/Lewis E. Gensler)
© 1934 by Paramount Productions Music Corp.
Assigned to FAMOUS MUSIC CORP. Warner/Chappell

The song might appear to be very long; but it is not. It has 32 bars, as do most standards. As the 8-bar sections A, B and D are practically identical, you only need to learn 16 bars: section A and the 8-bar bridge section C. It is the section in the middle of the song that changes over to D minor.

Here, too, it is essential to tap your foot. Pay particular attention to the crotchet rests at the beginning of a bar. The fact that the song is written in F major should not cause any problems. We do not need to think up any tricks to create more rhythm as the melody itself contains a strong bounce.

Now let us turn back to melodies with a quick tempo – in contrast to 'Love Is Just Around the Corner' – but in which the bars are filled with just one melody note. As a practice example, let us take the song from page 109, 'Whispering', and I set you the task of producing a rhythmic accompaniment throughout, using an alternating bass and other bass patterns as well as chords used in instalments. You will find that with the knowledge you have now acquired, this is relatively easy. For the first two bars, an alternating bass pattern, *c* - *g*, would be ideal. In the next two bars, with B^9 chords in the right hand, we will apply trick 2 and move the bass in ascending steps. The left hand then plays the following:

Of course we cannot use the C major scale as the basis for the ascending scale in the bass, it must correspond with the chord in the right hand as we would produce discords otherwise. As the chord symbol is B^9 and in B^7 and B^9 chords the seventh step of the B major scale is lowered by a semitone, we will use exactly the same notes in the bass: *b* - *c sharp* - *d sharp* - *e* - *f sharp* - *g sharp* - *a* - *b*.

Now let us look at the next four bars. For C^6 you could use the alternating bass *c* - *g* again if it was not for the *f sharp* in the right hand that would coincide with the bass *g*. So here we will use two *c*s as the alternating bass, one octave apart.

The next three bars do not need livening up at all as there are crotchets running through them. Then there are two bars with D^9 chords. You can use the alternating bass *d* - *a* in one of them at least and perhaps even continue it to the second, even though it contains crotchets.

There now remain six bars in the first passage. The first two of these have semibreves in the melody. Here we must think of something a bit different. Perhaps trick 17: break up the chords into their individual components and play them one after another. Let us look at these two and the other four in one piece.

220

In the last bar we will not go to too much trouble. We will repeat the two notes an octave higher, that is all. Now the whole thing is played again from the beginning. In the final two bars of C[6] we will take the bass chord apart, playing the notes in descending motion.

There are a great many such foxtrot melodies amongst the repertoire of standards in the same quick tempo and with the same note values: crotchets, minims and semibreves; melodies that need to be livened up rhythmically using the techniques shown. This is something that can easily be achieved with practice. You just need to develop a feel for when to apply a certain trick: the alternating bass, the step-wise ascending and descending bass, the bass that imitates the movement of chord elements in the right hand; or playing part of the chord in the left hand, followed by the rest of the chord in the right hand; or using repetition of one or two notes an octave higher.

221

As a test example I will now write down the verse of 'Whispering', giving the melody and chord symbols only. Please look closely at the melody and think about how and where you could liven up the rhythm.

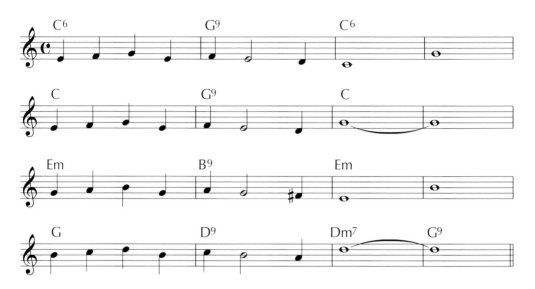

Whispering (J. Schonberger/R. Coburn/V. Rose)
© 1920 by Miller Music Corporation, New York
© renewed 1948 by Miller Music Corporation
Für D und A: Bosworth & Co., Köln – Wien

We can immediately eliminate the bars that have a chord on every crotchet beat as there we can play just the key note or an alternating bass. If there is just a semibreve in the right hand, we can move the bass in ascending or descending steps. Then there remain only the cases, such as in the second bar, where it would suffice to play the seventh interval in the bass, separately as two minims. And with this our harmonization is complete. So that you can check your harmonization I will give you the verse in a complete form, showing one way in which you could add rhythmic interest.

222

Whispering (J. Schonberger/R. Coburn/V. Rose)
© 1920 by Miller Music Corporation, New York
© renewed 1948 by Miller Music Corporation
Für D und A: Bosworth & Co., Köln – Wien

Please do not worry if your arrangement looks quite different. There must be at least twenty different ways of adding rhythm to the proceedings. It really does not matter whether you play the full C^6 chord or not in the first bar, whether you play the note *f* and *g* the other way round, whether the steps in the third and fourth bars ascend or descend.

For the B^9 and D^9 chords, we can add the third to the seventh interval. This saves notes in the right hand. Be careful in playing the E minor scale in the bass! You know that there are different minor scales. The important thing is to remember the second note, *f sharp*. For the rest of the scale you can use whichever type of minor you like best. Try out a few scales and different notes and listen carefully to whether they go with the right hand or not. Our ear is always the best judge.

There are many possibilities for the two final chords. You could use ascending or descending scales. Or, as we have done here, play the same chord in the left hand as in the right hand, but as a broken chord. In the last bar one note of the G^7 chord has gone for a wander, to end on an *a flat*. This means that the G^7 chord has become G^{9-}.

Until now in this chapter we have dealt exclusively with bringing a bit more rhythm into our playing. There are, however, many independent rhythms. I am thinking now in particular of the Latin-American rhythms, of which there are a great many: beguine, huapango-beguine, tango, tango-campera, canción ranchera, rumba, baion, merengue, merecumbe, chachacha, bolero, bossa nova, pasadoble, guaracha, mambo, samba, calypso, chunga, marcia, pachanga, baiao, montuño, la balanga, la cumbia, la carioca, la batacuda and others.

It is impossible to deal with all these in this book, even superficially. That would fill volumes. We will, however, at least have a look at four of them: beguine, rumba, chachacha and bossa nova.

These rhythms are played best and most cleverly by South American bands and they appear in many different variations. Of each of these four different styles, I would like to show you just two quite simple patterns, which are easy to play. These are by no means complete. They are intended to prepare you so that you do not play the wrong rhythm in a particular piece. You may also happen to play with other instrumentalists or singers who have such a song in their repertoire. It would then suffice to play the chords with these basic rhythms so that you can make a useful contribution to the band.

224

1. Beguine
Pattern A:

Those were C^6 chords. You will certainly be able to apply the same rhythm to other chords. In the bass you play three main notes of the right-hand chord. With Dm^7, for example, *d* - *a* - *c*, with G^7 or G^9, play the key note, the third and the seventh in the bass, i.e. *g* - *b* - *f*.

The most important thing is to play the rhythmical accents precisely, according to pattern A. You could play this bass pattern with different bass notes and even break up the right-hand chords.

You could even work in a 'break' by either having a rest on the fourth beat of the bar, or by playing a chord with both hands on

the first quaver of the bar and remain silent for the rest of the bar.

Pattern B:

This pattern, with the same rhythm in the left and right hands is used mainly when we are accompanying and do not have to play the melody. We can manage the chords quite easily in this style and maintain it for a long time without getting nervous or tired.

2. Rumba
Pattern A:

The secret of Latin American rhythms lies in the way the eight quavers of a bar are grouped and accented. In the rumba the quavers are formed in two groups of three and one group of two. The first quaver of each of these groups is always strongly accented. In the beguine, on the other hand, all the quavers are accented individually except for the second and third which are joined together as a crotchet and accented.

226

Of course you really have to concentrate to begin with, particularly when you have no rhythmic support and have to play the rumba all alone on the piano. It would be much easier if you were surrounded by a group of Latin American rhythmatists going crazy with their maracas, congas (drums for the basic rhythm) or bongos (also hand drums but higher-pitched and tuned in fifths), guiro (a kind of hollow wooden grooved instrument which is scraped with a wooden stick), claves (wood blocks), pandeiro (ring of bells) or tambourine. Then your hands would automatically move in a rumba rhythm, as if guided by magic.

All well and good! But what do you do if the rumba has a melody? How do you fit it in with all these quavers? It is really quite simple, you play only the bass line and, when there is space, add a chord in the right hand.

... and so on.

Pattern B:

3. Cha Cha Cha

Pattern A:

Here the quavers are grouped in a more straightforward way. Notice that in Latin American rhythms, in contrast to jazz and standards, the quavers are never dotted.

Pattern B:

4. Bossa Nova

The bossa nova is the most interesting and demanding rhythm of all, and the most complicated. This should really be incorporated in your playing as its tremendously rhythmic, yet calming, style creates a fascinating effect.

You can never fully create this when playing the piano on your own and you have to compromise. It is based on the samba and consists of three rhythms played by different instruments which fit together like cogwheels. For this reason a piano is not able to produce the complete inter-weaving of these rhythms. Another characteristic is that the rhythmic pattern is two bars long and so we have to look at sixteen quavers at once rather than just eight. The drums, for example, emphasize the quavers in the first bar differently to those in the second:

This relatively simple pattern is enough for most pianists. It is the same in each bar and thus does not observe the style of the bossa nova's sixteen-quaver pattern. In pattern B, on the other hand, we have incorporated this characteristic into the piano arrangement.

The bossa nova is also demanding in terms of its harmonies. It can happen in bossa novas that we come across chord symbols that we have never seen before. We find an example of this in the song 'Murmurio', in which the final chord is indicated as $Cm^{j7/9}$. At first glance this symbol appears absurd, because m (minor) and j (= major seventh) are right next to each other. But the first part of the symbol (m) refers to the lower part of the chord, the second (j) to the upper part.

Another chord that is often found in bossa novas, but one that we have already encountered, is the 11th chord, for example Db^{11+}. If you look back at pages 136 and 137 you will recall the essential elements. The second way of writing the notes and accidentals is the correct way.

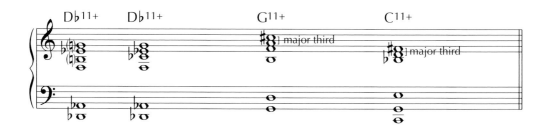

It is usually used in a much simpler form, which is much easier to play. As you can see above, you would normally have to play a tenth interval with a fifth added. So instead we play it like this:

Now we are faced with the question of when to use this chord. You will probably remember the module C - Gm^6 - A^9. The 11th chord is sometimes slipped into this module, to replace the Gm^6, producing a particularly distinctive sound. I will show you this module in the most commonly used keys:

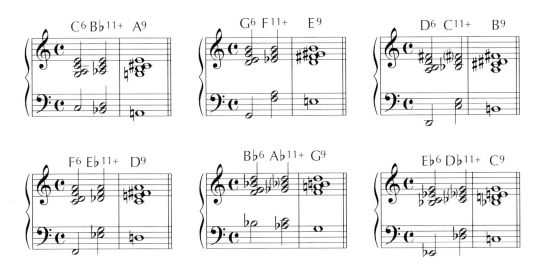

you will be working with such rhythms it cannot do any harm to learn some contemporary pop styles as well as standards. There is such an amazing diversity and finesse in modern pop music, which is often underestimated by older people. The whole spectrum of types of rhythm changes very rapidly. Some disappear and others appear.

That was the last chord – our chord-account is now complete. It really does not matter which way the rhythm goes, the chords are our important capital. They are just as important in all rhythms.

To finish with, we shall look at an arrangement of a disco rhythm that is as complete as possible. As the keyboard players amongst

I will show you examples of standard patterns of eight of the most popular disco rhythms: beat, slow beat, disco, funk, reggae, rock, salsa and soul.

1. Beat

Pattern A:

Pattern B:

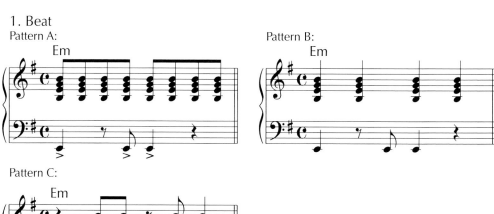

Pattern C:

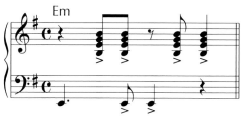

2. Slow Beat

3. Disco

4. Funk

5. Reggae

6. Rock

7. Salsa

8. Soul
Pattern A:

Pattern B:

You can now experiment with these eight rhythms and find different chords that fit in. With reggae and salsa there is a clear Latin American influence, which makes these rhythms particularly interesting.

A disco keyboard player needs another skill, which is that of being able to make up suitable riffs. A riff is a short, usually a two-bar, second rhythmic melody, which can be endlessly repeated and is intended to complement the main melody. The riff can be played by the lead guitar, rhythm guitar, keyboard or bass. It is an ornament that is somehow remotely related to the fugue. Let us take any melody for which a disco rhythm might be suitable.

To create a riff, we will write the notes of this melody in two stacks next to each other. In the first stack we bring together each note that belongs to the chord of the melody. In the second stack we bring together the rest of the notes that also appear in the melody.

We will take the three lower melodic notes for our riff. The components of a riff should be close to each other so that the same pattern can be used as far as possible when the chord changes, only higher or lower.

We will now add rhythm to these notes; in a different rhythm to that of the main melody, e.g.:

If the chord sequence now changes over to the chord of the fourth step (in this case C major), then it could be necessary to change one of the notes of the riff in order to make it fit with the new chord.

You can see for yourself that it is not really difficult to make up a riff that fits. With that we will leave disco music behind and turn to a few remaining questions. And these are: How do I improvise introductions to songs? How do I link one song to another? And, how do I create an ending?

1. *Introductions*

Four bars are quite enough for an introduction. We have a whole series of modules at hand to improvise such a four-bar passage. I will just select a few examples, which we will also use later for the transitions and endings.

a) Merry-Go-Round of Fifths module

b) chromatic module

c) 'exotic' module

d) normal module

You can see that we have enough raw material to create whatever is required. Let us now select a module that we can use from each type. With the Merry-Go-Round of Fifths module A^9 - D^9 - G^9, for example, we can create an introduction for a song in C major:

Merry-Go-Round of Fifths:

Chromatic:

Exotic:

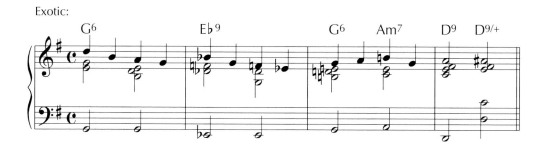

Normal:

The above examples provide enough modules for introductions, which you can vary as necessary. The next thing we need to know is how to link one song to another in a different key.

2. Transitions

Transitions should be as short as possible. It is best to bring in the seventh chord (in one of its variant forms) of the target key immediately. From C to F perhaps like this: from the final C chord of the old song, $C^{7/6}$ and $C^{7/+}$ take us straight to F major.

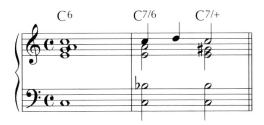

Or from C to G:

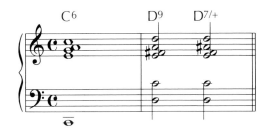

Or to a remote sharp key, for example, A major. The seventh chord of A major is called E^9.

Or to a more remote flat key, for example, Ab major. The seventh chord of Ab major is called Eb^9.

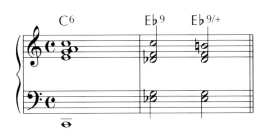

For the transition to the target chord the strongest magnet is always $X^{7/+}$ or $X^{9/+}$. The raised fifth step pulls the sound energetically to the key of the new song.

3. Endings

Two to four bars of improvisation are usually enough to complete a song. Our considerable supply of fillers enables us to create all kinds of closing themes. Here, too, we could take the Merry-Go-Round of Fifths, or form a chromatic ending or add exotic chords. Normal modules such as, for example, C - E♭° - Dm are also very suitable. I will show you an example of each and you can make up a few dozen others. The major seventh is often used as the very last chord. It has a distinctive and conclusive sound.

You will always succeed with this system of introducing or ending a song. You can also quickly master the rather more complex skill of linking one song in a particular key to another song in a different key if you proceed according to the previously-shown scheme: Find the ninth chord that leads directly to the target key and add the magnetically-acting $7/+$ or $9/+$ for extra support. This is the easiest and quickest way to reach the target key. So, two chords are enough to master any transition (modulation). It does not help and sounds rather artificial if you go through a series of modulations finally to reach the target. It is better to play a longer introduction to the song.

As you are now thoroughly familiar with the construction of chords and have worked extensively with all chord types, you will no longer encounter any unfamiliar chord symbols in your imaginary moving chord control band. You are now equipped to master any standard. It is clear that it is not possible to acquire the many techniques in a short time. But now all the tools imaginable are at your disposal, to enable you to work on the most diverse models and, in time, to perfect them.

In addition to the purely technical, there are also emotional moments, where the piano playing needs to be more expressive, where you need to add a bit of soul. If you frequent bars and clubs in which piano music is offered, you will notice that many pianists are technically absolutely brilliant, but their songs somehow do not reach out to the audience, they do not communicate well. Other pianists, however, do not perform complicated runs up and down, which usually actually pulls a melody to pieces. Neither do they carry out any amazing acoustic acrobatics. But oddly enough their music reaches out, often even directly touching the listeners' hearts. They bring so much expression, so much feeling into their playing that it sends out emotional waves and awakens memories, feelings of well-being, of contentment, or of melancholy.

This cannot be done with technique. There must be another way of achieving this. The first thing to bear in mind is that you can only give away what you actually possess. How can you communicate an emotion if you are empty of emotions?

This applies not only to pianists. All the great jazz musicians and interpreters – saxophonists, trombonists, clarinettists, use the same trick to bring expression to their playing. They do not just play notes … they play words! In other words, they tell the story of the song that they are interpreting. To do this it is necessary to obtain the text of a song and learn it from memory before beginning to play. The notes and harmonies might be fixed, but with exactly the same notation it would not be the same sound if the song 'Solitude', which tells of a person's loneliness, was called 'What a Wonderful Day'. The piano would suddenly have to portray a quite different story to express itself quite differently and to convey different emotions and the listeners would experience different feelings.

So to play the piano freely you also need to experiment with your emotions, to

239

speak the words in your mind with every single note or chord that you play. You will soon discover that this method works perfectly.

It is also clear that the words bring along their own rhythms, which have a much more powerful effect than the notated rhythms. Four quavers, three crotchets and a minim look like this on paper:

If you do not know the text, you would play it as written and it would not sound particularly interesting. If, however, you have the text that belongs here in your mind, your playing would immediately sound different. You would automatically colour the notes with the rhythm of the words 'Then what will they say about me?'. So you put yourself in a certain mood and, with the help of the piano, pass it on to others.

Processes such as this require experimentation over a long period of time; a description is not enough to make this clear. This applies to much of what you find in this book.

In the course of these chapters I have offered you all the techniques, tricks and tips necessary for playing the piano by ear. If you are still looking for chords or chord-modules of more unusual keys to use in your improvisations, modulations and variations, a module-table follows, with the help of which you will be able to master every conceivable task.

It remains only for me to wish you enthusiasm and joy of discovery in your forthcoming excursion into the land of free piano playing. I hope that all those who hear you play will be enchanted wherever and whenever you sit down to play the piano.

CHORDS, MODULES AND MODULE-CHAINS

C chords

G Chords

D Chords

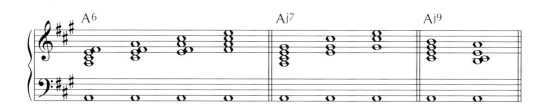

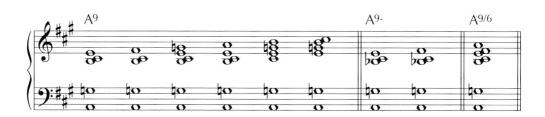

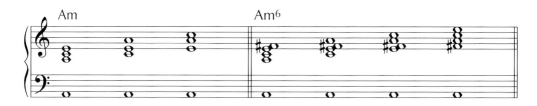

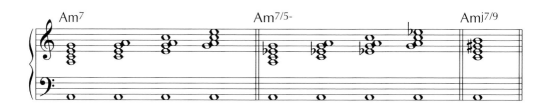

A Chords

E Chords

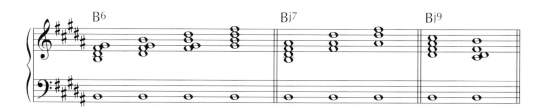

B Chords

F Chords

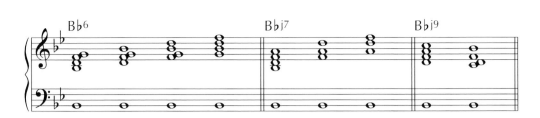

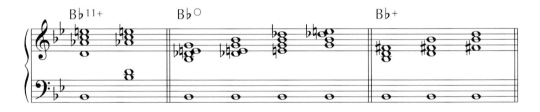

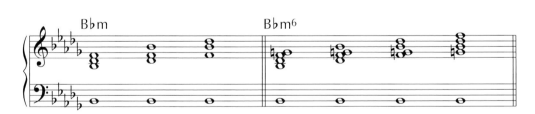

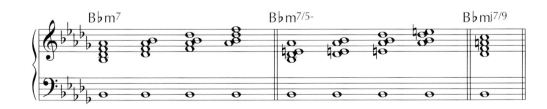

B♭ Chords

E♭ Chords

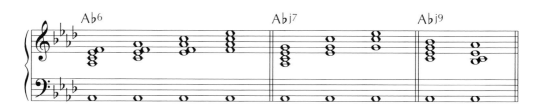

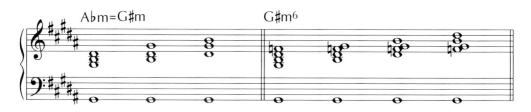

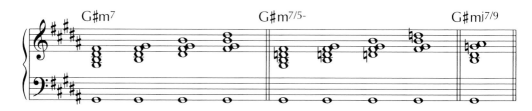

A♭ Chords

D♭ Chords

Gb Chords

MODULES
AND
MODULE-CHAINS

C Modules

C Modules

G Modules

G Modules

D Modules

D Modules

F Modules

F Modules

B♭ Modules

B♭ Modules

E♭ Modules

E♭ Modules

COPYRIGHTS

CD CONTENTS